This Is No Game: The Perils of Seeing Politics as a Sport

This Is No Game: The Perils of Seeing Politics as a Sport

Benjamin Darr

IFF
BOOKS

London, UK
Washington, DC, USA

First published by iff Books, 2026
iff Books is an imprint of Collective Ink Ltd.,
Unit 11, Shepperton House, 89 Shepperton Road, London, N1 3DF
office@collectiveinkbooks.com
www.collectiveinkbooks.com
www.iff-books.com

For distributor details and how to order please visit the 'Ordering' section on our website.

ISBN: 978 1 80341 992 3 (Paperback)
978 1 78535 626 1 (ebook)
Library of Congress Control Number: 2024951154

A CIP catalogue record for this book is available from the British Library.

Design: Lapiz Digital Services

UK: Printed and bound by CPI Group (UK) Ltd, Croydon, CR0 4YY
Printed in North America by CPI GPS partners

The manufacturer's authorised representative in the EU for product safety is: eucomply OÜ - Pärnu mnt 139b-14, 11317 Tallinn, Estonia, hello@ eucompliancepartner.com, www.eucompliancepartner.com

Contents

For Dad, who taught me sports, and Mom, who taught me politics.

When the chess game is over, the pawn and the king go back to the same box.

Irish Proverb

Acknowledgements

Writing this book would not have been possible without the support of Loras College, in the form of a semester-long sabbatical which I used for research and writing. I am indebted to Christoffer Lammer-Heindel for his encouragement in this regard, and for his willingness to read early drafts and offer helpful feedback. I also owe my thanks to David Carroll Cochran, because he also read much of the manuscript, but mostly for his unsolicited encouragement, his solicited advice, and for setting an example worth emulating. To Dan DeYoung and Clark Potter, I owe much, especially for Dan's insights on major league baseball, and for Clark's insights on top-level chess. I am grateful to Holly Darr and Nick Driscoll for keeping me on task throughout, and to Christine Darr, who offered early encouragement as well as the impetus to get this whole project kickstarted. Thanks also to Adam Smith, for last minute review and also for stimulating conversations that lent a particular shape to the argument of the book. And for various forms of personal support and inspiration, I also wish to thank St. John's Episcopal Church (especially Fr. Kevin Goodrich and Mtr. Susan Forshey), Alex Cohen, the Dubuque Chess Club, Joe and Bev Darr, Emily and Reed McCullough, and Neal and Miles Darr.

Acknowledgements

Introduction

Despite the appetite of those who read books on it, politics is not for everyone. Most people need to compare politics to something a little closer to everyday life in order to make sense of it. When it comes to American politics, sports analogies might be the most common way people do this. Phrases that tie sports to politics come to mind easily. A dark horse candidate. A layup. A body blow. The chessboard of world politics.

Americans routinely see politics through the lens of sports. And given the bad taste that politics leaves in most people's mouths, sports comparisons probably function as the spoonful of sugar that makes the sour medicine of democracy go down for the average citizen.

At first blush, this affinity between sports and politics seems to be just what the doctor ordered—after all, why shouldn't people liken democratic participation to a fun, healthy, agreeable pastime? There are certainly many upsides to thinking of politics as a sport. But this book asks: what are the downsides? More specifically, what characteristics of modern sports might lead our understanding of politics down a path that takes us away from our democratic ideals?

***

My interest in this topic stems in part from my own early life experience. In my adolescence I was a huge Detroit Lions fan. I idolized running back Barry Sanders and wide receiver Herman Moore, and watched each of their games whenever I could, even videotaping them for viewing again later. I cared so much about whether the Lions won or lost that it reached the point of irrationality. If some misfortune befell my beloved Lions in the middle of a game, I blamed myself: I shouldn't have stepped away from the television when I did; I should have cheered harder; I shouldn't have had those negative thoughts earlier. I recall praying some of the most earnest and fervent prayers of my youth just so that the Lions could win on gameday. Somehow it meant everything to me, even though it had absolutely no direct effect on my own life.

Such rabid fanaticism and superstition could easily be chalked up to the foolishness of youth and dismissed in order to move on to more serious topics. After all, today I can't name a single member of the Detroit Lions, and I'd be hard pressed to name many NFL players at all. However, following the Lions was a key part of my social and even political development, introducing me to conflicting group identities and conflicting agendas, and showing me how to care about something happening in the outside world. In fact, this was probably the first time I really cared about any events in the wider world beyond my social circle in the small town of Terril, Iowa. And these events did have an indirect effect on my social circle itself, as I was the only Lions fan in my school, with most of the other kids being Bears, Vikings, or Packers fans. As the lone Lion, I wrapped myself in sweatshirts, T-shirts, and jerseys, establishing a unique identity among my peers.

I played a variety of sports as a boy, and those were certainly edifying and character-building experiences. But I also watched a good deal of spectator sports on television. If this was my earliest introduction to the external world of politics, then what did it teach me about that world and how to participate in it? The first thing most mass audience sports teach us is to be spectators: to channel our activity into following the sport rather than participating in it. Interestingly, as we grow up, we end up playing sports less and watching sports more. These sports teach us to be fans: to remain loyal to our team and cheer for them through thick and thin. They train us to identify with an elite group and treat their victories as our own. The players of the game are the elite athletes, and we are there simply to watch them and cheer them on. The parallels to modern electoral politics are striking, and these will be explored in Chapter One, "Fanning the Flames."

Second, mass audience sports also teach us to be analysts and strategists: to pay close attention to the strategies of how to win rather than asking questions about, say, who should win, or for that matter, why winning is so desirable in the first place. Watching sports coverage that does this acclimatizes us to news media coverage that treats elections in the same way: the winners and losers here are the elite politicians who are competing in elections. Through this narrow lens we do not see the interests of business, labor, consumers, ethnic groups, or any other messy considerations of politics that may lie behind the politicians themselves. When politics is covered like a sport, the everyday people who are winners or losers in the realm of policy are obscured or even ignored, thanks to the exclusive focus on who is winning in the political *arena*. How the various politicians are polling, campaigning, and performing in debates takes precedence over their campaign platforms and how they would affect everyday people. The rise of "sabermetrics" in baseball interestingly parallels these developments in politics. I will examine these dimensions in Chapter Two, "The Tyranny of Strategy."

There is a particularly apt example of the tyranny of strategy in one of political science's most long-lived concepts: the median voter. This is the voter who sits in the middle of the pack of all voters on a left-to-right ideological spectrum. Standard economistic theories of electoral politics usually begin with this voter as the prize for which all candidates compete. Understood in this way, an election is simply a game in which each candidate strategically tries to capture the central ideological ground in an effort to maximize his or her own share of votes. Chapter Three, "The Meta-Strategic Median Voter," outlines and critiques this understanding of politics by showing how its hyper-strategic characterization of elections ultimately undermines democracy, even leading voters to falsify their own preferences at the ballot box. With insights from the 2016 presidential election, this is a useful case study of the tyranny of strategy discussed in Chapter Three, as it demonstrates how an excess of tactical voting and thinking can erode the functioning of democratic systems.

The book's final chapter draws out some broader implications of my critique of politics-as-sport. Particular attention will be paid to quantification, gamification, big data, and artificial intelligence, as these elements presently conspire to push society further in the direction of quantified managerialism. This chapter will also connect the book's argument with important social theorists, such as Max Weber and his concept of rationalization, René Guénon's definition of modernity as the reign of quantity, and contemporary thinker Paul Kingsnorth's critical analysis of "the Machine." In short, the gamification of politics, with its emphasis on strategic interaction, numerical metrics, and computer-calculated optimization, is part and parcel of the trend toward quantified managerialism in society writ large. Putting the problem into this larger context helps us to see its dangers more clearly.

Chapter One

Fanning the Flames: Politics for Passionate Spectators

Sports culture in the United States invites most people to be fans rather than players. There is a sizeable scholarly literature on the phenomenon of fandom, as it has become a prevalent mode of social interaction in online culture. In this chapter I aim to interrogate the phenomenon of sports fandom in particular, and how its dynamics can translate into approaches to politics that run counter to democratic ways of engaging in politics. In particular, fandom presents a model of public life wherein: 1) the expected role of the public is that of an audience that merely spectates and cheers for elite political players instead of acting in its own interests; 2) ordinary people build irrational affective ties to political elites as fan-objects and to their fandoms; and 3) social interactions, especially concerning politics, are largely limited to other members of one's particular fandom. Each of these fan-based attributes of sports culture is corrosive of democratic politics in its own way.

Drawing on the growing field of fan studies, the first section will discuss what it means to be a fan, and the related concept of a fandom, and apply these to the context of popular sports culture. The following three sections will each look at a distinct way that sports fan culture corrupts the nature of the democratic process. The concluding section addresses some objections to my argument.

Fans

Most American adults' experience of sports is that of spectators rather than participants. But what motivates people to follow sports? The obvious appeal is that, through spectacles of competition, mass sports events provide viewers not only with drama but with an unscripted reality that traditional fictional drama cannot provide: athletes are not play-acting, but are actively vying against others to the best of their abilities. But there are powerful social-psychological forces at work when people become sports fans. Two in particular are worth distilling here. First, it pays off socially to have something to talk about with one's friends, and something to watch with them. And our culture—especially men's culture—has long been saturated with small talk about recent events in sports. This gives many people an initial social incentive to start following sports. Second, and more unexpected for the uninitiated, is the intense feeling of attachment to a group and the vicarious thrill that comes from sharing the group's triumphs and tragedies. This second motivator does not come from simply following sports, but from identifying with a team and becoming a fan.

My own experience serves as an illustrative example here. I decided to get into sports in junior high school because all of my friends were, and of course I wanted to fit in. Wanting to stand out from the crowd of Bears and Packers fans, I picked the Detroit Lions, and found myself enjoying watching Barry Sanders and the Lions on a level I never anticipated: I recorded every game I could, I subscribed to the weekly newspaper *Lions Report*, and I bought an NFL football simulation game for our family computer and became coach of my own Detroit Lions team. I had enough Lions garb that more often than not I was wearing it.

Yes, I had successfully made the social inroads I was after: I figured out what all the other boys in school were talking about, and why, and I felt like I fit in. More than this, though, I had gone all in as a fan. Although being a football fan allowed me to fit in, my identity as a *Lions* fan allowed me to differentiate myself from the group. I even had a sense that this difference made me and my interests more interesting and more sophisticated than all those Bears fans. To this day I fervently maintain that Barry Sanders is the most exciting running back to watch in all of football history, and I am incapable of drawing a line between this objective truth and any partisan Lion bias I may still have.

The concept of a sports fan is so normal and mundane in American culture that it is easy to forget that "fan" is simply a shortened form of *fanatic*, or one who is "marked by excessive enthusiasm and often intense uncritical devotion." The word *fan* is also quite portable and is regularly used outside the context of sports: people declare themselves fans of certain movies, actors, directors, musicians, authors, videogames, and even of corporations or products outside of entertainment. The concept has suffused our casual language, for instance when one expresses that one is "a big fan," or on the contrary, "not a fan."

Why Sports?

If so many people are fans of so many things besides sports, then why do I focus on sports in particular as a frame for understanding politics? What makes sports a particularly powerful model for politics is that it is framed explicitly around competition, with clear winners and losers. Other forms of entertainment do not provide a competition framework that so closely parallels American politics as it is experienced by the public. Even when competition is injected into nonsports forms of entertainment—for example, in the process-of-elimination competitions of most reality television shows, or in videogame speedrunning—it is usually in the form of a multi-competitor race or a free-for-all competition. Examples such as *American Idol* or *Survivor* come readily to mind.

By contrast, the most popular spectator sports in the United States—think football, basketball, baseball, and hockey—are usually binary competitions between two and only two teams. This of course closely resembles commonsense perceptions of the basic two-party structure of American politics. This structural similarity helps explain why so many sports metaphors resound throughout political discourse. I could describe a particular political "play" by a politician as a "slam dunk," and I could describe a "move" by another politician as a "Hail Mary," (a metaphor that draws upon Catholicism for some and football for others) and virtually everyone would know the difference in meaning this implies. And everyone would know what I meant if I were to mention the Democratic Party's "full court press" against Trump, or the GOP's advertising "blitz" about inflation and other economic woes under the Biden administration. And we refer routinely to the political "arena," likening politics with boxing, or perhaps more aptly, mixed martial arts.

What makes these metaphors work is that they are situated in the context of a strategic struggle between two contending rival groups. As I will argue below, many of the assumptions about politics that are engendered by sports metaphors like these are incompatible with a democracy in which the masses (*demos*) act in their own interests to check the power of political and economic elites.

What Makes a Fan a Fan?

Following in the footsteps of seminal scholars in the field of fan studies (Jenkins 1992; Abercrombie and Longhurst 1998; Gray, Sandvoss, and Harrington 2007; Busse and Gray 2011), Ashley Hinck (2019, pp. 9–10) lays out four characteristics of fans. The first is the emotional tie fans feel with a fan-object, or in our case, the team. Fans feel an affinity and an identification with whomever or whatever they are fans of. This affective bond is foundational for fanhood, as it serves as the basis on which the fan's loyal relationship with the fan-object is built. This means that the fan empathically feels the thrill of the team's victory, as well as the sting of their defeat.

Second, fans cultivate a specialization of knowledge relating to the fan-object. Sports fans will not only come to learn the names of most members of the team, but their positions, their jersey numbers, and so on. Fans will often even track statistics such as rushing yards, batting averages, or three-point shooting percentages.

This wealth of specialized knowledge provides conversational fodder for the third distinctive trait of fans: their participation in a community of fans now known as a fandom. Since the rise of social media in the last twenty years, fan culture has exploded. As the internet expanded the possibilities of social interaction beyond previous geographical limits, people have shown a marked tendency to connect with other fans to discuss what they love about their fan-object. Thanks to the ongoing communications revolution, fanhood has also become normalized. Recalling the plot of the 1996 film *The Fan*, in which a crazed baseball fan murders a member of his favorite team for the good of the team itself, Sandvoss (2005) reminds us that "fan" used to be a somewhat derogatory term indicating extreme levels of enthusiasm falling outside of expected normative behavior. The online congregation of fandoms of all sorts and the resulting normalization of fanhood has marginalized such pathologizing narratives of fans as fanatics.

We may be tempted to think of fans simply as consumers: after all, the main thing that makes one a fan is what one spends time watching, reading, or listening to. But for the most ardent fans, these obvious and necessary consumptive fan behaviors are accompanied by productive behaviors as well: fan fiction, fan art, and the production of online discourse from forum posts to podcasts. Such productive (rather than consumptive) behaviors constitute the fourth characteristic of fans.

The bar moves a little higher as we move from the first to the fourth characteristic of fans. While virtually any fan has an affective attachment to the team and will watch and enjoy their games, only the more hardcore fans will participate in online discussion with other fans, or in other, more demanding creative activities. However, social media has made this activity more accessible and popular than ever before. Of course, necessary to all four of these characteristics is that fans enjoy these activities and engage in them primarily out of pleasure, rather than simply a sense of obligation (Hersh 2017). This being said, however, fanhood often *is* accompanied by a sense of duty or obligation—to support one's team, to watch their games, to speak up in their defense when needed.

There is now a sizeable scholarly literature in the interdisciplinary field of fan studies.

As noted above, two key observations of this field of study are that the rise and normalization of fandom as a mode of social relations has been spurred by development of social media, and second, that fans cannot be seen simply as extreme consumers, but as producers. This had led to a breakdown in the old distinction between media producers and consumers, bringing into being what Henry Jenkins (2006) called *convergence culture*. Convergence culture has come about as fans, through the internet and social media, have developed an increasing capability to influence the production of their favorite franchises, shows, and series. Cultural producers frequently come from the fanbase of the franchise they are hired to work on, and fans now have more means of making their voices heard by those in charge of writing and producing the shows. Convergence culture is likely more pronounced in the world of television and film, but the same trends have impacted the relationship between sports fans and the players and coaches they watch. Related to this, scholars have noted the emergence of culturally productive *fandoms*: the communities that frequently develop online around fan objects, from pop stars to television series to sports teams.

However, as in so many realms, scholarship in this area seems to have raised more questions than answers. What is the nature of the relationship between fans and their fan-objects? Between fans and other fans? How is power exercised within fandoms? What role does antipathy or negative affect play in fan communities (McCulloch 2019)? To what extent are people motivated by fanhood or, alternatively, by anti-fanhood (Theodoropolou 2007; Gray 2019)? Does fandom culture generally promote or stifle creativity and original thought? Does it all represent an enormous diversion away from substantive issues, à la Huxley's *Brave New World*, as Neil Postman argued (1985), or does it organize people into meaningful communities that can be mobilized and socialized into political life (Hinck 2019)?

The central question of this chapter is: has the recent rise of fan culture—and sports fan culture in particular—been a desirable development in the political sphere? It is only natural that fan culture would permeate politics, not least because people so often experience politics as a form of entertainment. But how does seeing one's role as that of a fan align one's expectations about politics? If sports fanhood in particular does serve as a sort of training for politics—as it did for me in my adolescence—then what does the process of becoming a fan teach people about political participation? What is expected of political fans, and what do fans expect of their parties and politicians? In short, how does the model of fanhood tell us to think about politics?

Fans in the Political World

My overall contention in this chapter is that fan culture serves as an undemocratic model for a politics that aims to be democratic. There are three main problems with fanhood applied to politics. First, fan culture considers the relatively passive activities of spectating and cheering for celebrities as the main way that the masses should participate, offering an anemic vision of mass politics. Second, fanhood exacerbates already all-too-human tendencies to loyally root for—and identify with—powerful people whose interests are usually opposed to the broader public interest. Finally, it divides the public into separate fan communities who forget how to talk to others outside their political fandom.

These arguments surely have their detractors. Many scholars have examined the impact of fan culture on politics. In fact, since one of the original motive forces of the field of fan studies was to recognize and celebrate fanhood, and to rescue it from patronizing and pathologizing narratives that marginalized fan culture, it is no surprise that many scholars have heralded the rise of fandom as a boon to democratic politics (Van Zoonen 2004; Jenkins 2006, p. 527; Hinck 2019). While there is substance to such claims, in my view most of the weight of fandom lands on the other side of the balance, and the turn toward fandom in politics represents an erosion of democracy.

Spectatorship: Passively Cheering On Elites

Fans exist to cheer others on. If we approach politics in the way a fan approaches football, then the role of the masses is first and foremost to get behind an elite group of celebrities and cheer for them. A similar conclusion could be made if we were looking instead at fans of a certain movie franchise, or a certain pop singer, or whatever. The point is that the role of ordinary people is to watch and cheer for those celebrities whose role is to actually play the game. This is an inherently antidemocratic impulse of fan-based politics. I am not arguing for a particularly strict, thick, or direct concept of democracy here. Even the most bare-bones conception of democracy requires that everyday people must not simply observe and cheer on their favorite politicians but must take active part in political decision-making processes. A willingness to take political action on the basis of one's own judgment is central to what makes one a citizen. By contrast, what makes one a fan is one's loyalty, support for, and identification with others who are the ones making the decisions and taking the actions for your entertainment. With regard to democracy, the problem here is not with sports per se, but with the concept of fanhood.

Participating in sports demands more skill than does watching them. So we might reasonably expect the first stage of training for participation to be spectating. But interestingly, our sports culture puts the cart before the horse here: participants in sports are overwhelmingly youth and children, and upon reaching adulthood, most people stop participating. And if they do remain interested in sports well into adulthood it is only as spectators. Although eight million American high schoolers play sports, only about one in fifteen of them will continue to play in organized sports in college in either the NCAA or the NAIA.[1] And according to a 2015 Harvard poll, while three in four adults played sports when they were younger, only one in four adults currently plays sports.[2] A similar trend of youth participation can surely be observed in other modes of performance, including music, art, and drama, where young performers transition into adult observers and fans.

If sports culture serves as a training ground for political literacy and citizenship, then this dynamic is detrimental to democracy. If, as a yard sign I saw recently said, democracy is not a spectator sport, then why does every other sport become a spectator sport once we leave school? Though children are active participants when young, we send them the message that growing up means sitting down and watching. Many have lamented the negative consequences of sedentariness for our bodily health, but insofar as sports is read as a metaphor for one's relation to public life, this is also unhealthy for our body politic.

Of course, it stands to reason that sports are particularly useful for the young, and some would object that growing out of sports allows young adults the space to grow into more adult concerns. This may be true in many cases and would be a powerful counterargument but for the fact that our sports culture centralizes mass spectacle sports, and the energy of participation in sports more often gets converted not into more mature concerns, but into sports fanhood instead.

Watching is fundamentally passive. This is not to say that watching a game of one's favorite team cannot be incredibly exciting. In my youth, I would watch my precious Detroit Lions games with fervor, and even record them to watch later. To be on the edge of my seat in the fourth quarter of a close game was a tremendously exciting experience. But despite all my eagerness, I was still just watching passively: the outcome was entirely out of my hands.

Interestingly, I did not believe this as I watched the games. I believed, against my better judgment, that my watching and cheering had an effect on the Lions' fortunes on the field. I knew of course that this was merely superstition, and given a moment's thought I realized that my actions had no bearing on the outcome of the game. Nonetheless, the illusion was powerful and at times impossible to shake. Perhaps the logic at the root of this superstition was that if the Lions' fate had such a powerful effect on my mood, the effect must somehow be reciprocal. Or perhaps it was simply wanting to rationalize by constructing some positive purpose to my excessive investment in the Lions' performance. Whatever the psychological reason for them, these superstitions nonetheless animated my behavior as I watched. Sometimes I even worried that if I stepped out of the room and missed part of the game, it would cause tragedy to befall my team.

The fundamental point here is that impassioned spectating *feels like* actively participating. A fan does not feel passive as he watches the game with intense emotional interest. Even if he *knows* better, he *feels* like an active part of the grand drama as it unfolds. This is the central appeal of spectacle, whether it is in sports or in politics: we feel, and are meant to feel, like a meaningful part of something bigger. In this way we *participate*—from the Latin, to take a part—in the spectacle. This could also be put forward as an explanation for why many fans feel compelled to produce fan fiction and other fan works.

It is now commonplace to identify both major sporting events and political events as spectacle. A spectacle is understood to be the commodification of mass communication into a readily consumable experience. The most influential theorist of spectacle was Guy Debord, who in *The Society of the Spectacle* (1967) argued that consumers are passive subjects that merely reify the commodified spectacle even as they attempt to critique it. Murray Edelman applied this logic directly to mass politics in the U.S., arguing that news reporting created a spectacle that "continuously constructs and reconstructs social problems, crises, enemies, and leaders and so creates a succession of threats and reoccurrences" (Edelman 1988, p. 1).

For those who were introduced at a young age to the mediated spectacles of popular televised sports, there is a natural connection to electoral politics. As a fan, you are first and foremost a spectator: it is your duty to watch the games, and to attend one or more of them if you are able. Putting in the effort to attend a game so you can root for your team in person most definitely builds your reputation as a faithful fan. You should loyally stand behind your team's star players and head coach, who represent the public faces of the collective fandom. This does not preclude the possibility of constructive criticism of the managers, coaches, and players, but it does mean that your loyalty is with them at the end of the day (McCulloch 2019).

Electoral politics can easily be viewed the same way. As a Democrat, it is your duty to watch the coverage on election night and root for the Democrats to win. Of course, you are above all expected to vote for them if you are able. And you should loyally support the star players, especially your team's presidential candidate, who is the highest public representative of the collective party to which you belong. Again, this does not rule out constructive criticism but does ensure loyalty in the end—you are expected to be a team player, after all.

Such analogies are nothing new. What I want to emphasize here is that this way of approaching politics produces a particularly anemic image of political action even while it presents it as a dramatic spectacle in which to take part. Just as adults generally stop *playing* the sports they love when they get out of school and instead adopt a spectator's relationship to sports, it is just as easy to adopt a spectator's approach to politics. This approach takes for granted that the celebrities we see in the media are the players and we are merely fans, and therefore the most meaningful way we can participate in politics is to vote for them, root for them at debate parties, and post on social media in support of them and in opposition to their opponents.

What this leaves out, of course, is any sense of direct political agency on behalf of oneself, or on behalf of any group that is not the team itself. The interests of the team of elite players are given priority, often even at the expense of the interests of the fans themselves. In fact, when the desires of the fans are too directly catered to by producers—for instance, when an excess of cameos are thrown into a reboot film just to make fans squeal with delight—such moves are derided by critics as cheap pandering or mere fan service. When politicians promise direct and straightforward actions in the interests of key voters, they are often similarly criticized by the pundit class. For instance, in the 2021 Georgia special elections, when Democratic Senate candidates explicitly promised voters $2000 pandemic relief checks if they were elected, conservative opinion-makers widely derided them for pandering to voters.[3]

What is common in both of these cases is that, although the purpose of the fan-object is ostensibly to please the fans, when this is done plainly and without subtlety as transparent fanservice, it is subject to criticism for a lack of artistic nuance. It is one thing for a politician to brandish the traditional rhetoric that she will work in the interests of the people or the common good. But getting too straightforward and concrete about this, such as by putting a specific number on the amount of money included in a relief check, is seen as insulting voters by appealing directly to their basest instincts. Along the same lines, the term *fanservice* originated in Japan to describe the common anime practice of explicitly sexualizing a character that fans have expressed a desire for (Barrett 2006). Giving the fans exactly what they want is an uncouth act, because it is aimed below the standards of art. In the same way, giving the masses exactly what they want in an unveiled transactional exchange for their votes aims below the standards of a decent public servant. Notice how seeing politicians through this fan-based lens approaches them as objects of art to be appreciated or criticized based on their own qualities, virtues, and rich layers of meaning and interpretation, rather than as a means to achieve policies in the interests of everyday people. While the former may sound laudable, it chafes against the substantive purpose of democracy by keeping the focus on the quality of the politician rather than the quality of life of the people. To be sure, both of these are valuable, but the politics of fandom gravitate strongly toward the former, at the expense of the latter.

As mentioned above, many scholars in the field of fan studies have noted the increasingly creative and productive role of fans and the consequent rise of convergence culture. Despite these very real developments, fans are still, in the final analysis, members of an audience. What makes fan production and fan critique notable is that they cut against this otherwise dominant grain—fan production is the exception that proves the rule that fans are first and foremost loyal consumers. Fan attention is focused externally on the fan-object, and fan communities exist only because they congregate around a shared fan-object. Without the fan-object, there can be no fans, and no fandom community. Even the most creative fan fiction starts with the raw materials given to fans by elite producers, otherwise it is not fan fiction but original fiction. Even the productive and creative impulses of fans are directed at furthering or improving the fan-object itself or its popularity.

Nonetheless, many scholars have observed that fan communities can be sources of political mobilization. Fandoms can direct their attention to social issues, as Ashley Hinck (2019) demonstrates with the case of the Harry Potter Alliance, a group of Harry Potter fans who mobilized against real social injustices, taking inspiration from the struggles for justice waged by Harry and his friends in the book series. Likewise, in the realm of sports, celebrity athletes often champion social justice causes. Before it got him blacklisted from playing in the National Football League, Colin Kaepernick's decision to kneel during the national anthem brought attention to police brutality and its impact on black Americans. Some high school and college athletes followed Kaepernick's example by kneeling as well.

Hinck investigates a more institutionalized example of activism among Nebraska Huskers football fans. Longtime Nebraska football coach Tom Osborne founded TeamMates in 1991, an organization through which Husker fans volunteer to mentor youth in school on a weekly basis. In analyzing the organization's recruitment drives, Hinck demonstrates how "Husker values" (Aden 2007) like the virtues of hard work, competition with rivals, and "joining the team" were all employed to inspire Nebraska football fans to get involved in youth mentoring (Hinck 2019, pp. 50–52).

Hinck argues that fandoms can serve as institutions of political mobilization, and can even partially supplant older, weakened institutions such as churches and labor unions. The Harry Potter Alliance and Teammates—along with other examples Hinck supplies—do demonstrate the possibility of all this, but they also tend to manifest a heroic politics in which people from higher social classes use their positions of influence to help those "beneath" them. This well-intentioned empathy politics is present to varying degrees in Kaepernick's activism and in the Huskers' TeamMates program, and is also illustrated in one of the chief examples of Harry Potter's own social activism: his rescue of Dobby the house-elf from his position of lifelong domestic servitude (Hinck 2019, p. 34). Harry and his friends take pity on Dobby from their relatively elevated social position and take the actions necessary to rescue him from his state of domestic servitude. Social action is reserved for Harry and his friends, as poor Dobby lacks the capacity, or perhaps even the will, to take action to free himself. This example serves to illustrate a kind of downward-looking empathy politics, in which only those with a sufficiently high class status are able to undertake effective and virtuous social action, and social action even becomes a means to prove one's virtue in order to shore up one's class status.

This kind of motivation for social action, which ends up reifying class inequalities, is certainly nothing new and nothing unique to the fan mobilization that Hinck documents. Indeed, the model of fan-based activism she highlights marks a hopeful and heartening trend for democratic participation, especially as more traditional and less transient community institutions like churches and unions are being continually weakened.

However, the inherent shortcomings of fan-based social and political action are significant. Firstly, a fandom is organized around shared "interests" (loosely speaking), but a labor union that represents workers' *material* interests against those of ownership and management is, politically speaking, a qualitatively different thing than a group of consumers uniting around a shared fascination in fantasy entertainment. Second, fan mobilization is always in some sense elite-driven mobilization and sometimes even amounts to elite manipulation of public opinion and political behavior through entertainment. After all, popular franchises have long been used to sell to their fans products of all sorts, and in this context a political party or campaign appears as just another such marketing effort, more astroturfed than grassroots.

More relevant here, however, is that even once we recognize the hopeful trend Hinck points to, the broader impulses of fandom tend to be undemocratic. While certain fandoms can be inspired by their fan-objects to join in political life in particular ways, the general idea of fandom as applied to politics is another question entirely. As Eitan Hersh (2017) has pointed out, when people participate in politics for gratification or entertainment rather than for duty or necessity—whom Hersh terms *political hobbyists*—they will tend to participate only in the more gratifying aspects of politics, including the stimulating impulse to take a side in an exciting contest. Here, as above, we see that the frame of fandom can make consumption of a political product—such as the "Wizards for Obama" T-shirt (Hinck, p. 23)—feel like active participation.

Given the way that fanhood so easily gives mere onlookers the illusion of active participation, it is worth noting that the problem here is not just the overall passivity of fanhood, but the deceptive way this is hidden from the fan. This accords nicely with Chris Hedges' criticism of twenty-first-century American culture in his book *Empire of Illusion* (2009, chapter V). In his own dramatic words, "the more we sever ourselves from a literate, print-based world, a world of complexity and nuance, a world of ideas, for one informed by comforting, reassuring images, fantasies, slogans, celebrities, and a lust for violence, the more we are destined to implode. As the collapse continues and our suffering mounts, we yearn, like World Wrestling Entertainment fans, or those who confuse pornography with love, for the comfort, reassurance, and beauty of illusion. The illusion makes us feel good. It is its own reality."

Loyal Attachment: Identifying with Elites

Even if one stops short of Hedges' critique of fanhood itself as a world of illusion, fan politics does construct a model of participation that is centered on spectating and cheering, effectively passivizing a citizen's conception of participation and subordinating it to elites who compete against other elites. Related to this is its second antidemocratic tendency: an emotional or affective attachment to elite celebrities, to the point that social identity groups are built around these figures. One of the main effects of this is to render elite interests as the fan's own, essentially disassociating the fan from her own best interests. Of course, the human tendency to divide into groups around leaders and to build identities around these long predates the rise of fandom and convergence culture. But fan culture and the associated rise of online echo chambers has certainly exacerbated this.

Part of what makes fanhood so exciting, especially in the world of sports, is the emotional attachment that a fan develops towards his team. As a fan in my own youth, I felt such a bond with the Detroit Lions that I rode high on their wins, agonized over their losses, and took personal offense at any insult to the team. I had a particular attachment to their most high-profile players at the time: Barry Sanders and Herman Moore. This is how a fan experiences his team: as though he is one of them. The previous section discussed how this translates into an illusion of participation. Just as importantly, this identification with the team builds an attachment that produces a fierce loyalty.

Sports fans are particularly loyal to their teams, when compared to other types of fans. The epithet of "fair-weather fan" is frequently thrown at those who join or rejoin the fan community only once the team becomes successful and withhold their support during difficult times (Gwinner and Swanson 2003). The pejorative nature of this moniker is corroborated by the finding that the more a fan identifies with his team, the less likely he is to dissociate himself with his team's failures, as a fair-weather fan would (Wann and Branscombe 1990). Sports fanhood is also typically more long-lasting than other types of fanhood, which can be based on much more transient cultural phenomena. With the exception of a few especially durable entertainment fan-objects (e.g., Star Wars, Star Trek, the Rolling Stones, and a few well-aged videogame franchises), sports teams and their fandoms are long-lasting compared to fandoms in other domains such as movies, television, videogames, and music. One can be born into a family as a third-generation Chicago White Sox fan, and this has very few parallels in these other fan domains.

As is true for other fans, sports fans tend to build social groups and even identities around their teams. This is especially true online, where fans can easily join other like-minded fans, but it should be noted that sports fan communities existed long before the internet thanks to their regional or local nature—Chicago of course is a concentrated community of Bears fans, Denver one of Broncos fans, and so forth. Even in a microsocial context, these fandoms can be powerful shapers or manifestations of social identity. Growing up, my loyalty to the Lions was unique among my friends, and often put me at odds with the larger groups of Chicago Bears fans, Minnesota Vikings fans, and Green Bay Packers fans, especially since all of these teams are longtime rivals to one another in their NFL regional division. While my following of football gave me a sense of inclusion, my support for Detroit kept my status as somewhat of an outsider in school. At the same time, it gave me a ready-made identity to wrap around myself, quite literally, as I mostly wore Lions clothing for several years.

This point should not be overstated. There are of course many other social identity groups that are more important and foundational than which sports team one is a fan of. But in terms of constructing a social identity, fandom presents a model that is of a particular character: fans look out for what is best for the fan-object, and often lose sight of what is good for themselves. The sports fan, in particular, wants her team to win, and when they do, she feels that she has won along with them. Sports fans will frequently use "we-language" (Sandvoss 2003), such as a Seattle Seahawks fan expressing joy that "we won on Sunday." This level of identification clearly implies the breakdown of the distinction between the fan and the fan-object: the fans are Seahawks just as the players are. This is identity in the categorical sense: I do not only "identify" with this team but am one of them.

That this sense of collective identity is centered on loyalty to a group of elites is what is worth emphasizing here. It was this process of fan-identity formation in my youth that served as a template for me to understand politics as I grew older. Most people who are invested in sports root for a particular team—that collective effervescence with the team is what makes the investment worthwhile. To be sure, there are other ways to be invested in sports: fantasy sports is one model that breaks with the traditional fan model, and this phenomenon and its political implications will be discussed in the next chapter. But the way most fans engage is a more straightforward emotional investment that takes the psychological form of a social identity with a collective group of fans, defined in opposition to one or more rival teams and their fans. Of course, as a young Lions fan I was not cognizant of this social-psychological pattern of identity formulation in any articulated way. But it is easy to see how this provided an unconscious blueprint for my later entry into politics.

These connections are not just an academic curiosity, but in fact are quite consequential to people's views of politics and what it means. In the world of spectator sports, when your team wins, you the fan win along with them. Translating this logic to elections is simple: political victory to a fan means that her party wins. Importantly, it does *not* mean that her standard of living increases, or that government policies change to her benefit, or even that her material interests (excluding of course her "interest" *as a fan* in her team winning) are earnestly fought for by her party. If the object of the game of politics is to win elections—if election night stands in for game night—then for the fan of a political team, all these other considerations are ancillary at best, and completely ignored at worst.

People come together to watch college basketball's elimination tournament during "March Madness," and they likewise come together to watch the elimination tournament of debates during the presidential primary season. People throw parties to watch the Super Bowl in early February, and they likewise throw parties to watch election night returns in early November.

In all of this spectacle, the real substance of politics—especially how it affects everyday people's lives—is all too easily lost as people sit in their living rooms cheering for their teams. With political victory defined for the masses as their team's victory on election day, and with so much of the electorate having committed to a team, the parties have less incentive to push through policies that benefit their fans in the mass public, because by the time the policymaking process begins, the spectacle is over and the fans have gone back home. The winners have no more demands to make—they have already won, and in their minds, their team clearly deserved it. And the losers will go home and start training for next season, confident that things will be better once they win.

Having fervently occupied themselves with the results of the election, neither of these sets of fans will be as engaged with the results of the governance that follows. With the exception of a handful of superfans or political junkies, most of the electorate will tune out during the off-season and start paying attention only once the spectacle returns. If they thought of themselves as players in the game of politics, perhaps this would be different, but spectator sports—and fanhood in general—habituates us to conceive of ourselves as fans instead: political victory is won on game day. Any attention such fans pay to politics in the off-season will likely be paid to the ups and downs of their team and its celebrity players in the news.

The team-based identities incubated by this model also encourage fans to look for differences between their team and the opposing team, and to ignore or downplay similarities. True fans want to believe that their team is special in good ways, and often as well that their rival teams are especially undesirable. This cognitive bias is rooted in motivated reasoning (Kunda 1987; Redlawsk 2002): a fan's thought process is aimed at an affective goal of affirming his preexisting identification with, and loyalty to, his fan-object. This motivated reasoning will necessarily downplay similarities that indicate that the rival team might also have good qualities, or those similarities that show that his own team might have the same faults as their opponents. When partisans exaggerate selective and morally loaded differences while downplaying similarities that cloud this clear moral contrast, it of course leads to stronger political polarization in the aggregate.

However, there are certain similarities between the parties that are emphasized by the sports metaphor: both teams are fundamentally pursuing the same goal, both are roughly equally powerful, and both are organized similarly in terms of their structure. When talking about the Democratic and Republican parties, such similarities are real and meaningful. But when politics is apprehended as a symmetrical contest between two roughly equally powerful teams who share all manner of similarities to one another in structure and purpose, broader political struggles are obscured or even ignored.

For instance, a game of basketball has little resemblance to the asymmetrical struggle of workers against owners and managers, for instance, even though the sport itself is filled with such labor struggles behind the scenes. A sports game provides a useful analogy for understanding the competition between the two major parties but does not analogize well to other important political battles, especially those which take the form of the many versus the few. The opposition between "teams" is important in that it displaces class opposition between masses and elites. As an example, the fact that employees (especially in the retail sector) are often called "team members" by their employers is a similar deployment of a sports metaphor to turn attention away from the hierarchical relationship between employer and employee, preempting class solidarity among workers with a push instead to be a "team player" in the rivalry between the company and its competitors. To the extent that struggles of the many versus the few are sidelined and politics is instead channeled into the two-party rivalry, partisan fans fail to see their own interests as citizens, subjects, or workers, and instead see the political interests of their party as identical to their own political interests. This is due to fans' tendency to identify with both their celebrity fan-objects and their fan community.

Much ink has been spilled criticizing the phenomenon of "identity politics," and I cannot hope to do justice to such wide-ranging debates here. What is relevant for us here is how processes of identity formation build affective ties between everyday people and elites. In a fan-based model, ordinary people build irrational affective ties both to political elites as their fan-objects and to other co-partisans as their fandom, and in doing so, neuter politics of its potential for improving their own lives over against those elites to whom they pledge their loyalty. Put most simply, the sports fan approach to politics displaces the solidary *we* of the masses in favor of a division into two *we's*, each of whom identifies with a different faction of the politico-economic elite.

Examples of loyalty to elite politicians come easily. The most obvious instantiations are when fans ignore problematic behaviors of their fan-object politician, and then opportunistically criticize another politician for similar behavior. For example, many Republicans were outraged at the Congressional spectacle of Christine Blasey-Ford accusing Supreme Court nominee Brett Kavanaugh of rape during their high school years decades ago, yet when Tara Reade leveled equally credible accusations of sexual assault on Democratic presidential candidate Joe Biden two years later, the same people were ready and willing to take such claims seriously because it suited their purposes. It is of course worth noting that the same example works just as easily in reverse for Democratic fans of Joe Biden.

Alternatively, fan loyalty is also on display when a politician does an about-face on an issue, and the fans of that politician follow, often seemingly without even noticing the contradiction. For instance, Democratic leaders Joe Biden and Kamala Harris publicly displayed their suspicions and hesitancy regarding the COVID-19 vaccines under rushed development by Trump's Warp Speed program during the 2020 election season. Then, after winning the election both Biden and Harris promptly reversed course on this issue once the same vaccines were given an emergency use authorization by the FDA. Fans of course followed, as reflected in the prevailing partisan split over hesitancy to take the vaccines.

Despite their loyalty, however, fans are quite capable of criticizing their own teams (McCulloch 2019) or their favorite shows (Baym 2000). McCulloch (2019) documents how criticism of one's own team is a central part of fan discourse and identity formation. However, there are limits to the amount of criticism—what he calls "fantipathy"—that is tolerated, and crossing this threshold will call into question one's membership in the fan community. Specifically, when the team loses, particular players or coaches are scapegoated, rather than blaming the team as a whole. Moreover, the poor performances of individual team members are called out only as temporary anomalies, not as permanent defects. McCulloch's analysis shows that, yes, fans are capable of criticism, but excessive criticism is policed by other members of the fandom: if the criticism "refers to permanent, unsolvable, and unmitigated problems ... the community should then respond with a resounding cry of 'You're not one of us!' The fan's criticism is not only rejected but Othered" (McCulloch, 242).

In a similar vein, Nancy Baym (2000) observes that fans of television shows are frequently critical of their shows, but nonetheless keep on watching. Viewers even go so far as to fast-forward through parts they did not like or reimagine a scene in a different way that is preferable to them. While fans are not uncritical of their fan-objects, it is rare for their criticisms to lead them to abandon their fanhood. Instead, such criticisms can be worked around creatively, and in the right context fans can use their criticisms to demonstrate knowledgeability and intelligence to other members of the fan community. For fans, though, rarely does criticism override their loyalty to the fan-object.

These are all quite familiar dynamics in politics as well. Consider, for example, the loyal Democrat who is willing to criticize his party, but only within certain parameters. He may criticize certain individual figures within the party as being corrupt or incompetent, but he will push back against similar criticisms of the party as a whole. There are temporal limits to his criticism as well: namely, public criticism is not appropriate during election season. And although he may be quite unsatisfied with the party, his loyalty prevents the thought of not voting Democrat from even entering his mind. That alternative would go against his very sense of identity. Instead, like the fan who fast-forwards through the undesired parts of the show, he will ignore the parts of the party he does not like, "hold his nose" and vote Democrat. Sometimes, such voters are so loyal to their party and their top politicians that they will even claim that all others who oppose the Republican party owe *their* loyalty and *their* vote to the Democratic party. Of course, this also routinely happens with partisan places switched as well. In either case, by this rationale an impulse of opposition gets turned into one of support, and the power to say no morphs into the obligation to say yes. This is not only undemocratic but inverts the logic of democracy itself: here voters are held accountable for their loyalty and support for politicians instead of vice versa.[4]

Separate and Polarized Fandoms

By presenting a passive spectator model of fan participation, and an irrational attachment to elite fan objects and their fandoms, the fan's approach to politics functions as a way for elites to coopt the interests of everyday people, allowing fans to imagine that when *their* elites win, they *themselves* win. But more than this, fan culture is also an important factor feeding into partisan polarization in the United States.

Lilliana Mason (2018) argues that when political scientists talk about polarization between the two parties in the voting public, this conflates two separate but related phenomena. The first is *issue polarization,* in which Democrats and Republicans grow further apart on their political values and policy preferences. This is what most political science survey research has measured and investigated under the rubric of polarization. Mason, however, emphasizes a second type: what she calls *social polarization*. This is when people feel more strongly attached to their identity as a Republican, or as a Democrat, or in some cases as a liberal or a conservative. This does not necessarily manifest itself in concrete policies, but in a comfortable and welcoming affect toward the in-group of one's own party and an exclusionary affect toward the opposing party. Mason frequently uses the analogy of sports to make the case that, because of rising social (identity) polarization, electoral victories are more important for most partisans in America than policy victories.

Mason makes her case carefully and convincingly, documenting through survey research that Republican and Democratic voters have become more socially polarized than ever before, at least since political scientists started measuring these things half a century ago. Moreover, the level of social polarization far outpaces the level of issue polarization that has occurred in that same timeframe. This has meant that more and more of people's social behavior is correlated with and predictable based on their party identity. Examples come easily: Democrats and Republicans increasingly watch different TV shows, shop at different stores, drive different kinds of cars, and listen to different kinds of music. All of this makes it easier to peg someone as a Republican or Democrat than ever before and makes it more difficult for partisans to find common ground with members of the other party, even outside the realm of politics. In Mason's own words, "more than just disagreeing, Democrats and Republicans are feeling like very different kinds of people" (29). What bears repeating here is that this is not accounted for by larger policy differences between the two partisan groups.

But why then has this happened? Mason catalogs a number of explanations, from the Democratic party's embrace of civil rights in the 1960s and the GOP's southern strategy in response, to the rise of cable news and media echo chambers, to the transition from a society minced by cross-cutting political cleavages to one that is increasingly bifurcated into two camps whose religious, cultural, and class makeup are each becoming more homogenous. Here I hope to put forward the incursion of fan-based approaches into politics as yet another piece of the puzzle accounting for our country's increased social polarization.

I wish to extend Mason's metaphor of partisans as sports fans rooting for their team. Spectator sports culture can serve as a training ground for the kind of identity politics that Mason conceptualizes. For many of us, this author included, sports were the first thing we cared about in the wider world beyond our immediate social circle. The only section of the newspaper that interested us for years was the sports section. We never watched the TV news, but we made sure to catch SportsCenter every night. Our conversations with friends at school would usually revolve around whichever major spectator sport was in season at the time: especially football, basketball, and baseball.

Recall that fans do not simply build an identity around their fan-object, but around the fan-community itself. In the case of sports fans, such identity building is often based in a team's hometown or home state. For instance, Red Sox fans build an identity not simply around their team, but the city of Boston and its regional identity. Huskers fans similarly construct their collective identity around what it means to be Nebraskan (Aden 2007). Green Bay fans famously wear large foam "cheese heads" to Packers games because cheese is a symbol of Wisconsin's identity. While sports teams latch onto these regional identities, at the same time having a top-level team to root for is also in itself a part of a region's or a city's identity. Thus, the country is sorted geographically into various sports-fan regions—regions which can vary depending on the sport but are still broadly consistent across major spectator sports like football, baseball, and basketball, especially for major cities: Chicago, Denver, Los Angeles, St. Louis, New York, Atlanta—each has its teams, and each serves as a hub for fans. Of course, there are diasporas of fans all over the country as well, but the regional pattern predominates.

Geographic patterns have developed in terms of partisan political identities as well. In what Bill Bishop (2009) refers to as "the big sort," certain cities and regions of the country have developed reputations and even local identities as either Democrat or Republican strongholds, as members of the two parties are socially sorting themselves into different regions, localities, and neighborhoods. Moreover, as discussed above, membership in one of the parties is often signaled by many other cultural and lifestyle characteristics, including religion, food preferences, and yes, sports preferences, to name but a few.

Thus, the geographical sorting noted by Bishop (2009) has been accompanied by what Mason (2018) terms social sorting, which consists in a lining up of different social categories such that it becomes easier to tell Republicans from Democrats based on their other social characteristics. The classical cross-cutting cleavages of political science no longer cut across each other like they used to, but instead cut the same direction to divide the American polity into two broad and diametrically opposed slices.

How does all this relate to fandom and its impact on politics? These social sorting processes have been taking place simultaneously with the rise of social media and the normalization of fanhood as a social relation and of fandoms as online communities. The model of a fan-based community is not only centered around celebrity elites but is also one in which the "community" is constituted of like-minded fans of the fan-object. As such, it presents a model of relations in which the preferred interactions are with those with whom the fan shares the preference for a particular fan-object. This brings a dynamic of insularity to fan-communities, such that people become accustomed to interacting with those who share their beliefs, and inexperienced and uncomfortable in engaging with others who do not. Thus the rise of fandom, insofar as it has modeled a mode of engagement in politics, is interwoven with the rise of online echo chambers.

However, fanhood also presents a model for how to engage with opponents. Fandoms—especially sports team fandoms—

often clash with online fans of different fan-objects. Just as fandoms congregate around beloved fan-objects, anti-fandoms can also sprout up around hated ones (Gray 2003). This happens frequently enough among fans outside of sports, but is especially common in the world of sports, where competitive rivalries mean that being a fan of one team often entails being an anti-fan of another. For many sports fans, disdain for an opposing team is often stronger than—or even the real motive force behind—loyalty toward their favorite team (Theodoropolou 2007).

How does this translate into poltics? Online political discourse can be read in the same fashion. Zeynep Tufekci (2018) puts it quite well:

> The problem is that when we encounter opposing views in the age and context of social media, it's not like reading them in a newspaper while sitting alone. It's like hearing them from the opposing team while sitting with our fellow fans in a football stadium. Online, we're connected with our communities, and we seek approval from our like-minded peers. We bond with our team by yelling at the fans of the other one.

Tufekci observes that our constant connection to others—especially to our fellow fans—structures our interpretations and our responses to the opposing team and their fans. Thus the social dynamics of online political discourse begin to resemble those of fans at the live sporting event itself. The (perhaps mythical) relatively disinterested and impartial newspaper reader is replaced by the engaged and partisan fan in the stands, who is just as likely to be motivated by hate for the opposing team than by love of his own team (or for love of the game, for that matter). Add this social dimension to the already mundane observation that many, if not most, partisans seem to be motivated by fear of the other party coming into power than by faith in their own party, and you have an accurate, if bleak, depiction of partisan polarization today. And as Mason demonstrates, this comes down to social identity more than policy issues.

This is not only a problem between Democrat and Republican partisans. Intraparty disputes are also frequently structured around fan-objects. This is most evident during presidential primary season, when candidates often receive backing from devoted online armies of fans. Sometimes these armies are a product of astroturfing efforts, such as has been shown to be at least partially true in the case of the "K-Hive," Kamala Harris's online following on Twitter during her 2020 presidential campaign.[5] However, the organic social processes of fan community formation are usually a bigger precipitating factor here, and these processes even exist when such movements are largely astroturfed. One important result of the "fanification" of politics has been the segmentation of different fan communities into echo chambers for each fan-object, such that people's political identities are structured around the politicians they support (or even around those they oppose). That more and more political interaction happens within the echo chambers of fandom of course decreases our capacity to understand our political opponents as anything besides opponents, toward whom we direct our vitriol.

Of course, all of this is to look at the problem from the demand side, so to speak. Matt Taibbi's book *Hate, Inc.* (2021) interrogates this problem from the supply side of the major news media, arguing that the rise of social media has given major news outlets incentives not only to choose a political side but also to use fear and hate of the other political side to keep viewers coming back. Just as Mason does, Taibbi compares the two sides to rival sports teams. From this angle, we might argue that news producers have been incentivized to present news and politics the same way that sports is presented in local news shows, cultivating among their viewers fanhood rather than critical citizenship, and expecting viewers to root for their team over their rivals. Although coverage of sports at the national level doesn't follow this model, similar patterns of partiality can be seen in local television coverage of sports, in which it is assumed that the regional audiences are rooting for the home team.

Objections

But what about all the positives of a fan's approach to politics? Fan culture, after all, has been celebrated by many scholars for breaking down the distinction between passive consumers and active producers. And some argue that fanhood is inherent to representative politics itself. For Cornell Sandvoss (2013, p. 288), fandom is necessarily how politics must be approached in an indirect democracy:

> The conflict between substance and form is one that originates in the very structures of indirect democracy. In representative democracies we vote for the form over the substance, hoping that they coincide to the largest possible degree. Political fandom is thus an inevitable condition of representative democracies – one that demonstrates its opportunities for participation and activism in a digital world as much as its inherent limitations, deficits and potential sources of disappointments and disenfranchisement.

If this is the case, then perhaps the rise of fandom indicates a more democratic politics. Perhaps fanhood's incursion into politics has somehow leveled the playing field by eroding the distinction between represented and representatives. If this means that producers listen to fans and must give them what they want, then what could be more democratic than this same thing happening in the realm of politics?

However, this rests on a misunderstanding of the relationship between a fan and the fan-object. The power to say no is fundamental here, and the political fan's strong identification with, and loyalty to, his politician, usually precludes him from credibly exercising this power. This is most often done, especially in American politics, through the claim that one should vote for whichever of the two major parties is seen as preferable. This claim is undergirded not by the logic of support, but the logic of prevention: we must prevent the opposing party from coming to power. By this logic, one should *vote against* the opposing party, rather than *vote for* the party you support. Perhaps this is best described as fantipathy: loyalty against, rather than loyalty to, a political party. This is an important and interesting extension of Gray's (2003) concept of anti-fandom. In any case, most partisans—whether loyal to their party, or loyal against the other party—can be relied on to back the "lesser of two evils" even when there are more preferable alternatives available. We will return to these strategic voting themes in the next two chapters.

In addition to this, the equation of representative democracy with the politics of fanhood also underestimates the extent to which what fans want differs from what is in the common good. If politics is viewed by fans as yet another entertainment spectacle to take interest in, as a drama with heroes to root for and villains to root against, then what fans want is to keep coming back to that spectacle for more entertainment (recall Hersh's political hobbyists). A fan wants victory, yes, but she looks for this only vicariously through the fortunes of her favorite political teams and players.

Moreover, fans might have more input in the creative processes of the entertainment industry than they did before the dawn of the internet, but they do not serve as the creators of their fan-objects. They are like moths attracted to a flame they did not light. Their presence may change the flicker of the flame, but not its placement or its basic properties. The concept of fan culture *presupposes* an elite production of fanworthy objects. In the world of sports, for instance, which cities have and do not have professional teams is decided by elites: powerful local politicians, large corporations, and wealthy owners. In politics, by and large, which politicians are put forward as candidates, and which policies those candidates can acceptably promote, are similarly constrained by the decisions of political and economic elites: party bosses, big donors, big business, and the like. Fans may have some traction with politicians, but most fans arrive at the show after the most important decisions have already been made.

Conclusion

Fandom does not push us toward a more democratic politics. Rather it continues to put elites in the driver's seat, and it does this very effectively. It convinces fans that they are getting what they want out of the system by inducing them to imagine that they are winning when in fact only "their" elite team is. It deceptively makes fans feel closer to the levers of power as they root vicariously for and identify with those who operate them. And in place of a common sense of community, it instead gives people a narrow sense of community among their fandom while they are alienated from opposing fans. In these ways fan-based politics exacerbates the difficulties of representative democracy and hinders a politics that serves the real common interests of everyday people.

Chapter Two

The Tyranny of Strategy: Politics for Analysts

> *We're an empire now, and when we act, we create our own reality. And while you're studying that reality — judiciously, as you will — we'll act again, creating other new realities, which you can study too, and that's how things will sort out. We're history's actors ... and you, all of you, will be left to just study what we do.*
>
> —attributed to Karl Rove (anonymously paraphrased by Ron Suskind)

As the previous chapter argued, sports analogies of politics lead us to think of members of the public as fans of elite politics. But how do they guide us in understanding the inner workings of the political game itself? In this chapter, I examine the ways in which sports metaphors make us think about politics as a complex game of strategy and tactics. While there are certainly parallels between sports and politics, this way of thinking presents us with several pitfalls that, much like the idea of fanhood discussed in the previous chapter, push our understanding of politics away from democracy and toward elite power.

I argue that conceiving of politics as a game of strategy does this in four ways. The first is to focus political attention narrowly on the strategy of elite political competition while losing sight of deeper normative political questions. Secondly, sports analogies tend to reify the established rules of the strategic game by avoiding foundational criticisms of the rules themselves and how they were made, instead directing our attention to whether the rules are enforced fairly or not. Third, this way of thinking builds a certain empathy for powerful elites by asking us to imagine ourselves in their strategic place as they compete with other elite political figures. Lastly, the supposedly intricate tactical complexity of the political game itself is frequently deployed rhetorically to deflect popular pressure. In the following chapter, I will show how each of these steers our thinking in practice, through the example of the median voter theorem and the overly strategic voters it tends to produce.

Winning Is the Only Thing

Legendary football coach Red Sanders coined the now well-known phrase, "Winning isn't everything—it's the only thing."[6] A good deal of American political discourse, especially during election season, consists of variations on this mantra. Candidates are constantly redirecting their speeches toward visions of their victory on election day, typically to the cheers of their fans. Presidential primary campaigns are often focused specifically, sometimes even exclusively, on the "electability" of the candidate rather than the desirability of their ideas and policy proposals.

This is a sensible way to approach sports, where the only thing at stake is the win itself. There are perhaps higher values that should be demonstrated in the effort to win, such as sportsmanship, etiquette, playing by the rules, being a positive role model for young fans, and so on. But the real outcome that hangs in the air is the victory or the loss itself. This is because the purpose of sport is to compete—a large part of what makes a sporting event interesting is that the pride of winning motivates players to train for excellence and play their best to pursue victory. In short, if Red Sanders is right and the point of sports is to win, this is because sports are designed for this end: may the best team win.

This is one place where the analogy to politics breaks down. In elections, of course, most would agree that there is much more hinging on the outcome than the pride of winning and the pain of defeat. State policy has real, material consequences in people's lives, and so does—one would hope—the outcome of elections. While the central end of sports is competition and the mastery it promotes, most would agree that the central end of democratic politics is not to find and cultivate and determine the best and most skilled politician, but for the government to govern in a way that broadly benefits the people it governs. As suggested in the previous chapter, thinking about politics as we think about sports leads us to pay fantastic amounts of attention to the election drama of conflicts, clashes, and competition, and neglect the actual consequences of government policy in people's everyday lives. Yes, of course winning matters in politics—but only insofar as it results in better or worse quality of life for a nation's people, and not simply for the sake of partisan victory in itself.

Of course, this is a well-recognized problem in media coverage of politics. Both scholars and pundits have critically examined the news media's "horse race" coverage of elections and its effect on our politics (e.g., Broh 1980, Iyengar et al. 2004, Patterson 2016). The hallmarks of horse-race journalism are well documented and well known. News media focus on which candidates appear to be winning or losing. Extensive editorial discussions are given over to how particular candidates are doing with particular demographic groups, especially racial groups and gender breakdowns. The most recent polling is constantly in demand and discussed the instant it is published. Who pulled ahead? Who fell behind? Did any dark horses surprise us? Is any candidate "punching above their weight"? (The reader will, I hope, forgive the mixed sports metaphors.) News coverage is characterized not by comparisons of candidates' policy platforms, but on how many delegates or states they have won, how they are polling, and especially any missteps they might have made on the campaign trail or tensions flaring up between candidates. Such mistakes and tensions are usually emphasized not for their policy implications, but for their personalistic nature. Perhaps the candidate was rude to her staff, or did something unsavory when in her youth, or stumbled when confronted in a debate. Missteps can cause a horse to lose the race, so they must be covered.

This type of coverage is particularly spellbinding among a pre-sorted partisan audience who is heavily invested in their team winning, and sports news coverage has played a role in bringing this about. Sports news served as a preexisting model which political news emulated as it tried to build its own fan base of partisan political junkies. "News purveyors knew: if they could find a way to cover politics like sports and get news consumers behaving like the emotional captives we call sports fans, cash would flow like a river" (Taibbi 2021, p. 190). It's not happenstance, then, that cable news coverage today falls neatly into Democrat- and Republican-aligned camps.

As for the academic realm, despite frequently joining in the choruses lamenting horse-race news coverage, political science has done its part in establishing the expectation that, for politicians, winning is the only thing. Rational choice approaches to political science have most commonly treated politicians as only interested in winning. Indeed, this seems to be a central default assumption to many analyses of congressional races. David Mayhew's classic book on legislators' behavior starts out with one basic assumption, that "United States congressmen [are] single-minded seekers of reelection" (Mayhew 2004, p. 5). This assumption, made by Mayhew in 1974, has become *de rigueur* in political science, which has borrowed the standard assumption of economics that human behavior is fundamentally motivated by self-interest, and that this singular motivation is the wellspring of all of the complex strategic interplay to be found in the game of politics.

There are of course many critiques of this game-theoretic turn in political science, and I do not wish to go into great depth on this topic here. The point is that when scholars of politics see it as a game played by strictly self-interested players, what we gain in parsimony is perhaps outweighed by what we lose: a sense of the real-life stakes of politics, including for all those putative pawns on the game board.

The Rules as a Given

But if winning is the only thing, what does winning mean? In each context this is of course determined by the rules of the game. In most sports, winning means scoring more points than the opponent(s) by the end of the game. Many sports deviate from this, such as tennis, in which you must win a certain number of sets versus your opponent, or golf, in which your score must be lower than that of any other competitor, but the rules are just as clearly established and the results just as easily quantified. Any sport can only be played with a universal agreement on the rules. The rules of the game may be debated, and may be gradually changed, but they remain the foundation of the game, on which consensus is necessary. For instance, the National Football League changed its rules by adopting the two-point conversion in 1994. Since the NFL is the officially recognized governing body that establishes its own rules for football, the game being played was still football, despite the rule change, and the change was accepted by the public.

While there may be debate about rule changes, and though some may oppose them, once a change is made, there is consensus about the new rules, and the players must abide by it. Though exceptions to this are newsworthy, they are rare. For instance, in the 1990s world chess champion Garry Kasparov, together with championship challenger Nigel Short, claimed that FIDE, the world governing body for chess competition, was corrupt and illegitimate, and broke apart to form the Professional

Chess Association (PCA), under which they played their world championship match. Under the PCA Kasparov continued to defend his title of world champion by winning a title match against Viswanathan Anand, while at the same time FIDE held tournaments to determine their world champions, since by their rules Kasparov and Short had disqualified themselves. The establishment of the PCA began a schism that was only mended thirteen years later, when PCA world champion Vladimir Kramnik defeated FIDE world champion Veselin Topalov in a world championship reunification match under FIDE, and today the PCA no longer exists. Boxing has also been subject to similar disputes. The history of sports is littered—but relatively sparsely—with other examples of rival leagues claiming rival champions.

But these are rare cases, and most of them temporary. The norm in the world of sports—and most importantly, people's everyday experience of sports—is characterized by a single hegemonic league—national or international—that establishes the rules and thus the true champions. The point here is that in sports, the rules of the game are only rarely disputed as rules themselves. Most often, they are assumed as a given. While there are endless disputes about whether a referee enforced the rules correctly in a particular case, disputes over the rules themselves are far less common.

We see a similar respect for the rules in politics as well, especially in mainstream liberal politics. It is evident in the widespread discomfort with changing the rules of the political game, such as abolishing the filibuster in the U.S. Senate, or packing the Supreme Court with more justices. Neither of these developments would violate the law, but both are commonly perceived as changing the rules of the game, and even as cheating. Such moves are seen as unfair play because players are changing the rules of the game in a naked attempt to win. Although winning may be everything, cheating is another matter entirely in the world of sports. As fair competition is at the heart of sports, cheating is the ultimate sin.

We also see this in how American media present politics in other countries when similar political moves are made. When a country's president leads an effort to amend the constitution so that he can run for another term (e.g., Russia or Bolivia in recent years), the dominant media frame for such efforts is one that characterizes such actions as cheating or as corruption of the democratic process, even when such moves are legal and have broad support in the public. Similarly, when the outgoing Venezuelan legislature dismissed several members of the Supreme Court in 2015, and when the high court declared the new opposition-controlled National Assembly in contempt of court, these were commonly portrayed as cheating in major U.S. media, despite these explicit powers of the Assembly and the Court being assigned in the Venezuelan constitution. This is perhaps because the courts are perceived as referees rather than players in the game of politics.

Similar to courts, journalists can be seen as referees of the game of politics as well, calling the attention of the audience to rules violations of the players. Thus, mainstream liberalism tends to react with alarm when politicians criticize journalists, such as when Donald Trump sharply criticized well-known reporters, such as in separate incidents with Jorge Ramos and Jim Acosta. Of course, the years-long imprisonment of Julian Assange for publishing information that governments wanted kept secret is another example, although one might have expected far more outrage about this than was ever present in the mainstream press. But this is the exception that proves the rule, since arguments against Assange typically characterized him as an illegitimate referee (journalist) rather than an official one.

The reporter's role as referee can be seen most clearly in the political spectacles that most closely resemble sporting events:

presidential debates. Convention now puts reporters in charge as moderators of debates, whose duties are not only to decide which topics get talked about and which questions get asked, but also to enforce the rules of the debate, including pressing a debate participant if she has not answered a question in a satisfactory way, or cutting off a participant if he goes past time. Natural as it may seem for debates to play out in this highly structured way, such was not always the case. Christopher Lasch traces the gradual historical shift from the Jacksonian ideal of politicians appealing directly to the public to the contemporary "journalistic interrogation of political candidates" (Lasch 1995, p. 165), arguing that the anti-populism of the mugwumps and the subsequent progressive movement transformed a political discourse that aimed to appeal to popular values and visions of a good society into a discourse that aimed to satisfy the demands of expert figures of authority.

Presidential debates have followed just this course, as affairs in which candidates freely debated each other on the vital issues of the day have now become more akin to oral comprehensive exams administered by professional, ostensibly objective, media proctors. Instead of free-form oratorial events, modern presidential debates, like sports, are highly structured competitive events in which rules are strictly enforced in real time. And of course, panels of reporters stand by to serve as Olympic-style judges who will deliver the post-debate verdict on the most important question of all—who won. In this arena, it is quite clear that the norms of spectator sports structure our expectations of political events.

Another way that debates resemble sports is in their conception of competition and fairness. Popular sports present competition as between two teams, and fairness in this context can be easily conceived of as balance between the two sides. This is also, of course, pervasive in our politics, dominated as it is by two major parties. From 1976 to 1984, the quadrennial

U.S. presidential debates were run by the League of Women Voters, an independent, nonpartisan group whose mission was to better inform voters. The two major parties then got together to form the bipartisan Commission on Presidential Debates (CPD), successfully displacing the role of the League of Women Voters, and organizing all general election presidential debates through 2020.

In the 1990s, Texas billionaire Ross Perot made two strong runs at the presidency from outside the two-party system, getting on the debate stage alongside the major candidates in both 1992 and 1996. In 1992, after being given equal time to deliver his message to the American people, Perot garnered over nineteen percent of all of the presidential votes cast nationwide. Although Perot's strong performance likely spoiled George H.W. Bush's reelection chances, neither party was happy with the prospect of an extra competitor. After Perot ran a second time in 1996—again making the debates, although with less success this time at the ballot box—the CPD instituted a requirement of 15% support across five national polls, and as a result, no third-party candidate has been able to participate in a debate since. This was no doubt intended. Whereas the League was a *nonpartisan,* independent organization with no connection to either party, the CPD was and is a *bipartisan* organization built by and for the two major parties, with a co-chair from each party.

The capture of our system of presidential debates by the two parties who directly dominate them is a patently and obviously undemocratic development. However, what makes the unfairness of this easy to overlook is a particular conception of fairness-as-balance that seems to have taken root in our politics. Under this conception, bipartisanship is seen as effectively and functionally identical to nonpartisanship. Since the CPD is neither unfair to Democrats nor unfair to Republicans, then it must be fair, the reasoning goes. Just as in popular sports, when there are but two teams competing at once, this standard of fairness suffices. But when this standard gets transplanted into the realm of politics, we can easily lose sight of those who are silenced by it—namely any and all third-party challengers.

Another parallel to this is the Federal Election Commission (FEC), which is headed by a board that has always been composed half of Democratic appointees and half of Republican appointees.[7] Again, this is the same deceptive standard of fairness, as despite the law being written in such a way that no more than half the commission can be from the same party, in practice this of course results in three Republicans and three Democrats. This may be fair to the two major parties, but effectively shuts out any outside voices or interests. When we view politics as a sport in which two teams compete, such problems can easily escape our notice. As a result, basic standards of multiparty democracy, such as the right for newly formed political parties to compete in elections, fall into jeopardy.

The Twisted Empathy of Strategy

Spectator sports naturally invite us to imagine ourselves in the shoes of the players and coaches. One result of this is a vicarious satisfaction in our team's victory and a felt sting of defeat in their losses. This personal identification with the fate of one's sports team was extensively discussed in the previous chapter.

But interestingly, despite the irrationality of our attachment to a team of strangers, our rational faculties are often fully employed in that imagining. Remember that one of the key characteristics of a fan is a large and specialized knowledge base (Abercrombie and Longhurst 1998). Fans are often impeccably informed and up-to-date concerning their team and its members, they often know the minutest details of the rules of their sport, and they deeply understand the particular strategies employed by the coaches of their team, and even those of rival teams. Fans will frequently criticize coaches' strategic choices and imagine that they themselves would have made better decisions. "If I were coach, I wouldn't have blitzed on that down; I knew it was too risky." The whole industry of fantasy sports has been spawned as an outlet for, and a way to profit from, these hyper-knowledgeable armchair coaches, who revel in role-playing as coaches and managers themselves.

This identification with players, combined with a focus on strategy, results in the supplanting of a sense of ethics or sportsmanship by technical competence and the choice of the right strategic move. If a tennis player delivers an angry tirade and shouts down an umpire for a line call he disagrees with, he risks being disqualified from the match. However, fans of that player will often sympathize with and defend the player's actions. Common rationalizations in such a case might include "I couldn't handle that kind of high-pressure environment either," "I'd have done the same, the judge had it coming," or even "if he didn't speak up there was nothing stopping that judge from continuing to make bad calls against him later in the match." Notice first that these justifications already have the fan imagining himself as the player. But also take note that in the final example, strategic considerations are used to justify a rank case of bad sportsmanship. Not only does the fan's irrational attachment produce the emotionally motivated reasoning it employs to justify the player's "Mac Attack," but the irrational, offensive act itself is interpreted as evidence of the player's rationality; in particular, evidence of strategic skill, and not hotheadedness. In assuming the player's rude conduct to be part of a long-term strategy, the fan conveniently replaces the player's unsavory vice of poor sportsmanship with the virtue of strategic cunning.

This is an example of a twisted empathy that seeks to understand and even justify bad behavior by viewing it through a predominantly strategic lens. The role of strategy is key here, as it allows one to interpret otherwise ethically questionable acts instead as shrewd long-term calculations to better ensure victory. Popular sports fans are particularly prone to this, especially those whose minds are filled with sports statistics, strategic plays, and fantasy football team rosters. The combination of the allure of strategy on the one hand, and the identification with successful and famous athletes on the other, draws them into sports fandom. This combination is fertile ground for a strategic sense of empathy with the players and coaches.

Among those who play competitive table games for entertainment, the same Machiavellian logic is common as well. "That play you made early on just to shut me out of any chance of winning the game—it made the game horrible for me! But I would have done the same thing in your position—nice play." In the context of a friendly postgame conversation among equals, this is nothing but good sportsmanship from one who lost a tough game.

But this same charitable interpretation takes on a different tone when set on the unequal field of politics, resembling a kind of Stockholm syndrome in which the loser gazes appreciatively upon the strategic mind of one who crushed his dreams. Imagine: "You know, although it ruined my retirement, I thought that your decision to cut our employee pension fund was, strategically speaking, exactly the right move in order to maintain our company's competitiveness in the market." Or, "Although it was your promise to push for a higher minimum wage that earned my vote, I have to admit that your later abandonment of that promise was a smart decision to keep the support of the manufacturers, and one I would have made in your position too." When such important things are at stake, such comments sound not only implausible but unthinkably obsequious and submissive. But if we liken politics to an amoral and recreational game in which winning is the only thing at stake, this is what can result.

Sometimes the questionable act in need of justification does not necessarily have to be seen as strategic itself, but it is instead enough that the player is recognized for his greatness at the game. Here character faults are simply forgiven, or even seen as the price of greatness. Returning to our hypothetical tennis example, such a justification might sound something like: "Say what you will about his temper—that doesn't change the fact that he's the best to ever play the game." There is little that distinguishes this deflection from the argument that might makes right. Here raw skill and competence supersede any questions of morality, such that one's greatness buys one indulgences for any number of sins. Paeans to Henry Kissinger's great strategic genius carry a similar tone—"never mind the human costs in Cambodia, Indonesia, et cetera... you've gotta hand it to him—the guy sure knew how to strategically triangulate!"

Under this way of thinking, skill, competence, and strategic cunning operate as stand-ins for ethics—technical skill in politicking and decision-making displaces the moral goodness of one's decisions in themselves. Thorny normative questions with ambiguous answers are neatly subsumed by tidier questions of measurable, quantifiable results: winning records, championship rings, batting averages, electoral victories.

This manner of analysis often gives media figures plenty to talk about with an air of objectivity, without being seen as taking sides. But at its heart is the desire for a neat numerical world free of moral ambiguity, a world in which the right answers can be judged by their strategic efficacy and their probability of success. Analytics replaces analysis, and all can look at the numbers and agree. This is a technocratic *realpolitik* which effectively discards ethics and replaces it with skill, with the predictable result of justifying the actions—whatever they might be—of those in power, because of the mere fact that they were able to stay in power. And this outcome is predictable once "winning is the only thing" is extended from sports to politics.

Sabermetrics and the One Right Move

We live in a world that is now inundated by and even structured by "big data," and it is interesting to note that data analytics came of age by being applied to sports. Michael Lewis's 2003 book *Moneyball* marked an important moment in baseball when the tried and true collective wisdom of managers was shown by quantified econometric approaches to be more tried than true. Both the statistics and strategy of baseball have been significantly impacted by the advent of data analytics, which in baseball is called sabermetrics. Sabermetrics has replaced many of the traditional measures of player skill, such as earned run averages and batting averages.

Sabermetrics' insistence on statistically quantified strategy has led to the making of management decisions that are not only counterintuitive, but in some cases diminish the drama and fan enjoyment of the game. The most high-profile example of this was Tampa Bay Rays manager Kevin Cash's removal of pitcher Blake Snell in the sixth inning of a World Series game against the Dodgers. Snell had pitched a remarkably strong five innings, allowing only two singles, and accumulating nine strikeouts. As a result, the Rays held a narrow 1-0 lead. Cash pulled the pitcher on the basis of sabermetric data: he believed the "one right move" was always not to let a pitcher pitch a full game. Ironically enough, in the final few innings, the Rays did not score any more runs, and the Dodgers scored three, coming back to win the game 3-1. Needless to say, Snell was not happy, and neither were the fans.

Even if it was the "right" call statistically speaking, it went against the proud tradition of baseball, and even against the spirit of sport itself. First, no traditional manager would have pulled Snell after such a stellar performance in the World Series, especially considering that his pitch count was relatively low, as he was not only striking batters out, but striking them out quickly. But Cash made the call because he was committed to sabermetrics. He made the move the computer told him to make. But more than this, to pull out Snell—especially when he wanted to keep pitching—violated the competitive spirit of sports, which rewards strong performers. Baseball fans will never know how the game would have ended if Snell had been given his chance to finish the game. Judging by the strength of his pitching that night, he should have been given that chance.

Another example from the world of baseball is "the shift" of infielders to one side of the field when the numbers indicate that a particular batter always hits that direction. This was never done before the advent of sabermetrics, but quickly increased in popularity in recent years. It is surprisingly effective, and consequentially slowed down the pace of the game by shutting down power hitters—typically baseball's biggest stars. It deadened the game enough that Major League Baseball recently had to ban the practice. "The shift" is part of a broader trend in baseball that many fans have observed: data analytics has taken much of the excitement out of the game. This is thanks in part to sabermetrics' excessive focus on achieving the "three true outcomes": homeruns, strikeouts, and walks. All of these are outcomes in themselves and are not subject to fielding errors. They are also less interactive, and generally less exciting for fans than the rest of the game, which involves fielding hits and throwing out runners.

Sports represent a world in which data can rule supreme, precisely because it is a world which is designed for the success of strategy. Sports are designed such that we can give credit to the skill of the winners at the end of the game, rather than blaming it on an outside factor. This is the whole point of sports: may the best team win. Strenuous efforts are made just so that outside factors, such as doping, do not corrupt the purity of winning by one's own efforts. In this environment, freed as much as possible from the whims of chance and the statistical noise that chance generates, data analysis can be a powerful tool. Football coaches can run the numbers on how successful each play is. Baseball managers can fine tune their batting lineup with piles of data representing each hitter's record. Data analysts have never been more strategically important in sports.

A similar trend has swept political campaigns in recent years. Data analytics tells politicians where to campaign and how to shape their talking points. It breaks the public down into segments that politicians can strategically choose to target or write off as unreachable. An expert class of consultants, big data at their fingertips, has taken over the way that political campaigns are run. It's no coincidence that Nate Silver, who is known mostly for his analytics work on presidential elections, got his start analyzing baseball. Although his website *FiveThirtyEight* is named for the number of electors in presidential elections, ESPN bought it and now features Silver analyzing both sports and politics. Silver is perhaps the most well-known member of the political data expert class.

One major consequence of the rise of the strategic experts of democracy is the mystification of politics for the masses. If politics is a complex strategic affair, to do it well demands the efforts of trained professionals who can read the tea leaves of public opinion surveys, internet polls, focus groups, and all manner of data that can be collected for strategic use. This puts the expert class in the active position of researchers and the public in the passive position of research subjects. Everyday people are merely the objects of the strategic game, as it seems they do not have the expertise necessary to play. This outlook not only makes participation in politics seem difficult and intimidating, but it makes even the observation of politics demanding. When politics is layered with strategic complexity, or at least perceived as such, it appears a challenge just to make sense of the political world—particularly for the untrained. Deference to elite experts is often the result.

Thinking about politics as a complex strategic game also nudges us to supplant technique for ethics, and to discuss politics as a game of optimization rather than deliberation. There is but One Best Way to optimize one's winning chances in a complex game of strategy. And the recent history of chess, that most respected of games, has taught us that strategic complexity calls not just for experts, but even for sophisticated algorithms built to navigate those complexities.

Around the turn of the century, chess computers became better at chess than the strongest players in the world. Since that time, the gulf has widened between humans and machines, as both computing power and the design of chess engines has advanced. Most recently, the best human-designed chess engines, which were "taught" how to evaluate a chess position by human programmers, have been dramatically outplayed by machine learning artificial intelligence engines such as AlphaZero and Leela Chess Zero. Such a program is not taught any criteria by humans other than the rules of the game itself, and it simply learns the game by playing chess against itself repeatedly. In the span of four hours, AlphaZero played itself enough to learn how to beat the strongest human-built chess engine, Stockfish. So thoroughly have computers gained chess dominance over humans, that now the computer programs which teach themselves to play are beating the programs which humans have taught to play, even when they are outgunned in terms of calculation depth.

One consequence of the computer revolution in chess is the ubiquity of the idea that there is one right move. Serious chess players looking to improve have always analyzed their own games. Now they usually analyze them with an engine, meaning that the search for the right move now comes with a "correct" answer in the form of the engine's choice. Human analysis before computers was often debatable, uncertain, and ambiguous. It was akin to writing a persuasive essay. With the dawn of the computer authority, it's now more like a math problem. Sure, showing one's work is still important, but the answers are readily available in the back of the book. Qualitative differences of style or taste in terms of how best to play in a given position—these can now be all too easily settled by a computer evaluation, which will tell authoritatively which side has the advantage, by how much, and which move is deemed the mathematically best move to play.

We see this idea of one right move in other forms of competitive gaming as well. In both video gaming culture and table gaming culture, players frequently speak of "optimal" play, or "the correct" move, even in games with random chance built in. Poker players, Magic the Gathering players, Starcraft players, Super Smash Bros. players—gamers of all sorts use this language despite the fact that these are far from perfect-information games. Additionally, the entire subculture of videogame speedrunning is built on the exacting premise of speed optimization, which produces a clear metric for determining who has the "best" run of any given game. Some competitive gamers even use eye-tracking software as they play, and the software will tell them not only where they were looking at different points during the game, but also where they *should* have been looking, and how quickly their eyes *should* have been moving.

This way of thinking about games—that there is one correct way to play, and anything else is "suboptimal"—turns otherwise open-ended and expressive diversions into engineering problems to solve. It is the same trend of rationalization Max Weber identified in the world of work, which subjected the workplace to the all-encompassing quantitative metrics of efficiency. Frederick Winslow Taylor was the most prominent advocate for such an approach to running a factory, searching for the "one best way" through what he called "scientific management." In doing so, Taylor ended up micromanaging the most minute physical motions of individual workers.

The one-dimensional Taylorist logic of factory efficiency seems to now be taking hold in the world of recreation and games. By this logic, a chess game must not only be won, but won optimally. We look to machines for judgment on this, often losing sight of ways to play that are instructive, artistic, creative, or simply more fun. And just as with the Taylorism of the industrial era, this subjection to efficiency is a result of the unbounded pressure of quantified competition.

While there are other critiques to be made of this general development, the point that concerns us here is that game players are now more accustomed to turning to specialists or even to computers for advice on how to play their games better. This demand for expertise and strategic knowledge has also been created by news coverage of sports: endless punditry bookends and suffuses all sorts of sporting events, most of which is characterized as expert analysis. The recent rise of fantasy sports also manifests the same demand for a specialist's proficiency—and now even algorithms and so-called artificial intelligence—to tell fantasy sports fans how to make their picks.

Here the connection to politics becomes evident as well. We hear constant evaluations of politicians' success or failure, their skill or incompetence as campaigners, from pundits who are put in front of us presumably because they have the technical competence to make such judgments. And they do so with access to mysterious data, using impressive quasi-academic jargon which splits the electorate into the most narrowly parsed intersectional voting blocs, described with such labels as "suburban soccer moms," "men without a college degree," or "middle-income second-generation nonwhite Hispanics."

On the one hand this may make politics seem more accessible, as it comes to resemble an entertaining pastime like sports. However, insofar as it tells us that understanding politics requires the aid of trained specialists, it does the opposite.

We see this most clearly in how it gives politicians a strategic rationale to hide behind when they disappoint their most ardent supporters.

Twelve-Dimensional Chess

One particularly striking example of this happened in January 2021, during a brief movement that was known as Force the Vote. A variety of notable progressive media figures pressured "the squad"—the handful of left-progressive members of the House—to withhold their votes for Nancy Pelosi as Speaker of the House on the condition that she promise to hold a floor vote on a bill expanding Medicare to all Americans.[8] Online commentator Jimmy Dore was the first to propose the idea, which was also supported by Kyle Kulinski, Krystal Ball, Briahna Joy Gray, Nina Turner, and Cornel West, to name a few important figures on the left.

Advocates of Force the Vote claimed that if the squad withheld their votes, they could pressure Pelosi into conceding to that demand, as Pelosi then would not have enough votes to win the speakership. Alexandria Ocasio-Cortez, the figurehead of the squad and its de facto leader, publicly dismissed the idea on Twitter, despite her many earlier indications that she would "cause a ruckus" in the Democratic party, and would be willing to spend all her political capital—even to the point of losing reelection—to accomplish exactly the kind of progressive agenda for which Medicare for All is the centerpiece. In the end, each member of the squad voted in support of Nancy Pelosi, without any such strings attached to their yes vote. By contrast, as soon as Republicans took control of the chamber in 2023, House Republicans in the Freedom Caucus used their leverage to gain substantive concessions from incoming Republican Speaker Kevin McCarthy, something which just a couple of years earlier progressive Democrats refused to do.

Ocasio-Cortez took a lot of criticism from the left for this seeming act of capitulation to Pelosi, who is perhaps the person who most symbolizes the corporate-serving establishment of the Democratic party. After all, Pelosi is one of the richest and most well-connected members of the House, with immense fundraising ability, and this gives her enormous power in the upper echelons of the party.

Ocasio-Cortez, in responding to criticisms that she had essentially sold out Medicare for All for her own legislative career, argued that her critics did not appreciate the strategic realities of the situation. She claimed that she and the squad had already gotten other concessions from Pelosi behind the scenes, specifically a deal on raising the national minimum wage to $15, another central plank of the progressive platform (and a policy which never did materialize). She claimed that if Pelosi were not elected, then Republican leader Kevin McCarthy would gain the Speakership. The fact that both claims turned out to be false is beside the point here, which is that both were used to try to demonstrate that the dispute she had with her critics was not about the value of Medicare for All, but about the strategy of how to get it done. Above all, she argued that the time to push for Medicare for All was not now, but later, that a certain strategic patience was required, and that her critics were aloof from the calculated complexities of the long game she was playing.

Of course, strategic considerations are important when pushing for any policy in any political context. But whether one finds Ocasio-Cortez's defense compelling here or not, this is a clear example of how a politician—even one who ran on a platform of standing up courageously for bold progressive policies—can muddy the waters of politics by talk of strategy and smart tactics. Despite the unique opportunity a crisis like Covid presented to make a strong push for Medicare for All, and despite the newfound political leverage of the squad,

Ocasio-Cortez still made the claim that the moment was not strategically right. Such rhetorical moves, as here, are usually employed to backtrack on campaign promises. Through this mechanism, politicians are able to convince their supporters that they agree with the policy in question and are doing everything in their power to bring it about. The disagreement is not about the ends to be achieved, they say, but about the means to achieving them; putatively they don't disagree about policy, but merely strategy.

This is an age-old political tactic, to be sure, but it gains more purchase in a world in which expertise is seen as necessary to navigate—let alone govern—bewildering bureaucratic systems. And just like the Weberian rationalization of sports and games discussed above, this too has at its root the scientific management characteristic of Taylorism: its emphasis on efficiency and its insistence that there is one right way. In Ocasio-Cortez's arguments, there is one correct way to win Medicare for All, and there are very smart qualified insiders, who, perhaps with the help of computer modelling, can organize the political forces in the proper, most effective way. Under this model of politics, a people's movement cannot simply apply pressure on government, they must apply this pressure under the proper expert guidance and supervision so that strategy can be optimized. The less-than-democratic nature of such a model of democracy is immediately apparent.

Of course, people are not always fooled by politicians' smarter-than-thou strategy talk. When people do object to politicians doing just this, what's notable is how quickly they turn to strategy games in order to form their objections. Critics will commonly lampoon politicians for playing three-dimensional, four-dimensional, or even twelve-dimensional chess. When such images are invoked, it is nearly always with a sarcastic and dismissive tone. After all, a politician who invokes the 3D chess defense is banking on his audience buying into his own political shrewdness, but it may be an open question whether making this move is itself so shrewd. In any case, the idea of deep, informed strategy has provided cover for countless politicians to effectively backpedal on their stated noble goals, and more broadly, to present themselves as authorities to be trusted and admired by voters, who don't share their strategic political skills—after all, they are the ones who got into office in the first place.

Conclusion: The Perils of Strategy

The game of politics is certainly a complex one, and surely involves a good deal of planning, strategy, and know-how. But we must not take this metaphor too far. This chapter demonstrates how an emphasis on strategy exhibits a tendency to push away from democracy and popular sovereignty, and toward elitism and expertise. First, treating politics as a game often means an unhealthy obsession with the question of who is winning, as the frequently bemoaned phenomenon of horse-race political coverage testifies. Second, when we think of politics as a game, we tend to take the structure of the game and its rules as givens. This also leads us to think of fairness under these rules as fair to all if they are fair to both teams, a mistake which is easily refuted but all too infrequently noticed.

Third, strategic acumen can easily come to displace normative goods like wisdom, virtue, and dedication to the common good, and lead us not just to identify with elite players of the game (as noted in the previous chapter) but even to valorize their cunning at exactly their most Machiavellian moments when they are playing the game only in their own interests. Finally, the bewildering tactical complexity of politics as a game creates an artificial demand for trained experts to tell us the right way to proceed, and this same complexity is frequently employed as a rhetorical trick by politicians scrambling for meritocratic justifications for their failure or even refusal to deliver on their promises to their constituents.

From Machiavelli's *The Prince,* to the immense influence of game theory on political science today, strategy has always played a large role in the study of politics. It's important to note the limitations of strategic analysis, however. The most notable is that understanding politics as strategy assumes that political actors each have goals that are simply given and unquestionable. How these goals came to be the actors' goals is completely outside the purview of game theory, which takes preference formation as a black box that it cannot and will not interrogate. The social and cultural origins of individual preferences—much less individual conceptions of the good—cannot be examined when game theory as a mode of analysis considers each actor as a discrete entity whose self-interest is both formed and understood as separate from that of others.

Strategic approaches to politics are narrowly concerned with how the game can be won, to the exclusion of questions of *what* should be won or what it might *mean* to win. It understands politics as a sport: the contest must be won according to the rules, and each participant can be understood as motivated by nothing else other than winning. In such an environment, dialogue, deliberation, and persuasion have no roles to play whatsoever. For instance, in sports, as in game theory, it is ridiculous—or at the very least egregiously against the rules—to imagine that one can win the game by persuading some members of the opposing team to switch sides. To attempt to do so by outside influence, as was done in the infamous 1919 World Series when members of the Chicago White Sox conspired to lose the series to make money on the betting markets, is one of the cardinal sins of sports because it corrupts the otherwise pure competition of sport itself.

While it has always been a cardinal sin in sports to try to "turn" one's opponents—or for that matter, to allow oneself to be turned—similar prohibitions seem to be in place in many subcultures of politics today. Take the recent presidential campaigns of Bernie Sanders as an example. Sanders was publicly criticized by many high-level Democrats for his official designation as an Independent in the U.S. Senate, the argument being that he was not really on the team because he was not a real Democrat. When Sanders held a town hall in which he advocated for Medicare for All on Fox News, despite the applause that Sanders garnered from a seemingly conservative in-studio audience, many progressives felt angry—even betrayed—that Sanders had dared even to go on Fox News for the event. This bears emphasizing: rather than being glad to see a persuasive advocate for Medicare for All given a chance to speak to the largest audience in cable news in order to change the minds that need changing, many on the left were instead upset that Sanders was legitimating Fox News by gracing their network with his presence. Under this interpretation, Sanders was working with the enemy and corrupting the purity of political competition between teams. He was colluding with the enemy, perhaps even to throw the game. Such a perspective prioritizes maintaining the purity of competition over the actual material interests of regular people. That such criticisms came from those who claim as leftists to fight for the interests of everyday people illustrates the perils of excessive strategic thinking which looks critically at means but not broader ends.

Another example of the same phenomenon can be routinely found in media discourse surrounding America's various wars, which also tends to exhibit the same obsession over means rather than ends. Coverage often emphasizes the strategic acumen of the generals, or the technical sophistication of weapons systems. Critiques of the strategy and tactics of the war effort are easy to find. But what may appear to be extensively critical coverage of a war actually expresses tacit support for the war itself by limiting its critique to the strategic means through which the war is executed, while the war itself and its ends are very rarely if ever questioned (Solomon 2007). Many scholars have argued persuasively that such narrow frameworks of debate provide the illusion of free and open discourse in major media, effectively disguising their propaganda function (Parenti 1986, Herman and Chomsky 1988).

However, the sharpest point here may be the contrast between the role of the analyst, who is ultimately powerless, and that of the player of the game. Perhaps this point was best made by Karl Rove, who saw himself and other top officials in the Bush administration as the players of the game, and plainly condescended to the journalists who offered their many critiques of the war in Iraq. "We are history's actors... and you, all of you, will be left to just study what we do." Even the critical strategic analyst is passive and powerless compared to the players of the game. Or even worse: the very act of deeply analyzing the decisions of the powerful puts them on a pedestal of Machiavellian ingenuity, tacitly acknowledging their might and extolling their cunning, wittingly or unwittingly. Perhaps the zenith of the tyranny of strategy is to have us look upon tyrants as triumphant strategists.

The next chapter will present a more specific case of the tyranny of strategy, one which stems from a longstanding pillar of political science and is now quite prevalent in popular understandings of U.S. politics: the median voter.

Chapter Three

The Meta-Strategic Median Voter

After Joe Biden announced his candidacy for the presidency in April 2019, the *Washington Post* ran an editorial which argued that he had better chances of being elected than most of his fellow contenders.

> Biden's virtue in both contests [the primary and the general election] is his relative moderation. He stands to the right of the bulk of his putative Democratic competitors, someone who has not built a career as a paladin of progressive policy priorities, as Sen. Bernie Sanders (Vt.) or Sen. Elizabeth Warren (Mass.) have done. But he stands to the left of President Trump on a host of issues. If the median American voter is like Goldilocks — in search of something not too left, not too right, but just right — Biden is well positioned to be her choice.
>
> —Henry Olsen, "Trump's greatest threat has arrived," *Washington Post*, April 25, 2019

This serves as an excellent everyday articulation of what is known to political science as the median voter theorem (MVT). The underlying assumptions of this well-known idea are that 1) each voter has a specific preferred place on a single, meaningful left-to-right spectrum of policy positions, 2) each voter will vote for the closest available candidate to their own position in either direction on that spectrum, and 3) voters are arranged in a normal distribution on this axis, with most of the voters clustering around the bell curve balanced around the political center. This particular understanding of politics—which not only includes a concept of how voters choose, but also strongly implies a recommendation of how candidates should campaign—is so popular it seems like little more than common sense in American politics today, as Olsen demonstrates here.

This chapter uses the MVT to demonstrate some of the dangers of applying strategic analysis to politics that were discussed in the last chapter. Conceiving of politics through the strategic lens of MVT can lead to the neglect of important normative questions, it can reify the rules of the game by focusing instead on how to operate most effectively within them, and it builds more empathy for the elite players of the game than for the voters who judge their suitability. But the fourth pitfall is perhaps best demonstrated here, as the median voter approach has time and again been weaponized against candidates proposing bigger, more meaningful policy changes. The way the MVT does this is by presenting status quo centrism as more strategically apt than more ambitious appeals to policy change. For all these reasons, the median voter theorem is a particularly illustrative case study of the tyranny of strategy.

Once the assumptions of the MVT are internalized, they subtly carry their logic from one election to another. Returning to Olsen's editorial, he claims Biden's moderation to be a virtue in both the general election and the primaries. Applying the MVT to a general election is relatively intuitive, especially in the simplified two-party contest that the American system produces. Voters feel they have a choice between two alternatives, and it makes sense that they would choose whichever candidate has what they perceive to be the closest match to their own political preferences. More importantly, general elections (especially in presidential years) turn out a large chunk of the electorate, and it seems a reasonable assumption at the outset that this large voting public would cluster around the middle of the ideological spectrum.

But why would Olsen claim that Biden's moderation is an advantage in a *primary* election? It's obvious that under MVT assumptions, moderation is advantageous in the general election, but Olsen says this moderation is a "virtue in both contests," including the primaries. However, most states have closed primaries or caucuses, in which only registered Democrats can vote. Also, since they fail to receive as much media attention and public visibility as general elections, far fewer people turn out for primary elections, and this means that the voting population in a primary will be comprised more solidly of high-information voters, who are more highly partisan (Brady, Han, and Pope 2007). With these factors in mind, the average group of Democratic *primary* voters bears little resemblance to the group of general election voters in November. Indeed, if it is easier to mobilize more progressive and left-leaning voters in a primary, moderate candidates may be at a disadvantage for having such middle-ground positions. So again, what is the logic at play in Olsen's argument?

Although it is not spelled out clearly, perhaps we can infer that Olsen's support for Biden in the primary is *meta-strategic*: its strategy is contingent on its expectation of others acting according to the same idea of strategy. Olsen is assuming that voters operate on two key assumptions here. First, they expect that some candidates will not be able to win against Trump and they would only support a Democratic candidate that they think can win the general election. This first assumption seems reasonable, but the second is more questionable: that voters assume that something like the MVT will hold true in the general election, therefore they would rather nominate the candidate that is closest to the general election's median voter. So Olsen not only believes the MVT to be true, he's also assuming that primary voters share in this belief and will vote strategically based on it.

Note that when these additional assumptions about voter behavior get layered onto the median voter theorem, the logic works backwards, spreading from the general election to the primaries. We need a candidate who is electable, and the MVT tells us who is electable. Thus, working backwards from MVT assumptions about the general election, the median voter theorem spawns the *meta-median voter* in the primary, who assumes that the goal of a primary election is to nominate someone who will satisfy the presumed median voter of the general election. Note that this is decidedly *not* the median Democratic primary voter behaving as such, but instead the primary voter's hypothetically imagined *general election median voter* that is operative here. This is why I call such voters meta-median voters.

We have here what Robert Putnam (1988) would call a two-level game, and the expectations of the second level game (the general election) influence the strategy of the first level (the primary election). Somewhat absurdly, we could even extend this reasoning one more layer if we were to imagine pre-primaries to determine who competes in the primaries: under this logic, meta-meta-median voters would feel compelled to select someone that was electable in the primary and the general election, and thus they would, again, pick someone moderate, so they could win the meta-median voter in the primary, and then the median voter in the general.

In this way the MVT acts as a self-fulfilling prophecy: if people believe it, and act accordingly, then it makes itself true by making its influence felt not at the level of the general election directly, but one step removed in a strategic sense at the primary election. Because voters can be led to think that moderation is what wins elections, then they can be led to vote for moderates even in primaries, and even when they would themselves prefer that a more progressive candidate fill the office. The result of this is that moderates get nominated in primaries regardless of the empirical validity of the MVT in general elections, and all that it requires is a *perception*—right or wrong—that this is how general election voters will behave.

It is not that Olsen supports Biden's policy agenda, but rather Biden's policy agenda is one that the median voter will support in November, under the assumption that the general election will be fought over the median voter. Perhaps Olsen's first choice based on policy stances was Biden, or perhaps he preferred a different candidate—we do not know, because his argument is not about his own preference, but simply about strategic considerations of who can win in November. This stands as an example of the dangers of strategic analysis: "winning is the only thing" loses sight of any goals beyond "our team" winning the election. It also represents well the idea of fantipathy: for Olsen, whichever Democrat wins the nomination does not matter, and what does matter is to keep Trump from winning. What Biden promises to do once he's in office is only mentioned in the context of whether that makes him a strong competitor or not. If MVT's assumption that more moderate (however that is defined) candidates are automatically stronger competitors in a general election is true, then this argument may hold some water. But this assumption may not be true, as suggested by, for example, the success of Donald Trump in 2016 and 2024, or that of Barack Obama in 2008.

If moderation does win elections, then we saw the underside of this logic—that extreme positions will lose elections—in the "pied piper" memo from the 2016 Hillary Clinton campaign. This was an internal memo written in April 2015 that argued that the campaign should "force all Republican candidates to lock themselves into extreme conservative positions that will hurt them in a general election." The memo stated that the campaign "[doesn't] want to marginalize the more extreme candidates but make them more 'Pied Piper' candidates who actually represent the mainstream of the Republican Party" ("Strategy on GOP 2016ers"). It included a list of such candidates, in which of course Donald Trump figured prominently. Here we see a tragicomic example of the failure of the median voter theory as it was applied by top-level presidential campaign staff who strategized to elevate the candidate from the opposing party who would go on to win the general election. Two months after the campaign's pied piper strategy was circulated internally, its fate was foreshadowed in the United Kingdom. Conservative Prime Minister David Cameron's bright idea had been to hold a referendum on Brexit that June, to take the wind out of the sails of those hardliners in his own party who were pushing to leave the European Union. Cameron's logic was the same as Clinton's: the median British voter surely wouldn't vote for such an extreme proposition. Both of these embarrassing and ironic failures of the median voter theorem came in remarkably quick succession, ringing wakeup calls for establishment moderates on both sides of the Atlantic.

MVT's Many Weaknesses

It's not just these recent events which have undermined the MVT as a way to make sense of elections. There is a vast and longstanding literature in political science that by now should have given the MVT a death by a thousand cuts. Attacking from a theoretical angle, Stokes (1963) uncovered several assumptions of MVT that are deeply problematic when applied to the realities of politics, including, but not limited to, several unsupported assumptions: that there is a single political dimension, that this dimension is stable over time, and that the distribution of individuals over this spectrum is similar in both Congress and the electorate. Other classic works have shown that there is little empirical basis for the MVT. Converse (1964) famously demonstrated that most voters don't think of how they vote on a coherent left-right spectrum, although admittedly this may have changed somewhat in the intervening sixty years. Romer and Rosenthal (1979), in a wide-ranging literature review, conclude that the preferences of the median voter had no significant relation to the government's economic policy. By the end of the twentieth century Fiorina (1999) lamented the demise of the moderating median voter model of politics and the rise of party polarization in its place. More recent contributions to the scholarly assault on MVT include Montagnes and Rogowski's (2015) finding that moderation does challengers no good in contests against incumbents, and Hassell's (2018) fascinating conclusion that party leaders are more likely to favor moderate candidates when the general election will be *uncompetitive* rather than competitive. This last finding suggests that to the extent moderation is valued by parties, it is not typically for concerns of electability.

Perhaps the most damaging empirical challenge to the median voter theorem has been the disconnect between public opinion on concrete issues that can be plotted on the left-right spectrum, on the one hand, and what is commonly seen as the political "center" between the two major parties, on the other (Hill and Tausanovich 2015). When public opinion is measured on concrete policy issues, polling data on bread-and-butter economic issues consistently put the public significantly to the left of this putative "center" (Drier 2017). For example, the 2018 General Social Survey found that the public thought the federal government was spending too little on education (77%), assistance to the poor (71%), health (70%), drug addiction (69%), protecting the environment (68%), and social security (57%) (GSS 2018). What makes this even more surprising is that a plurality of Americans identify as conservatives, when the other options are moderate or liberal (Saad 2017).

This contrast between the bipartisan political center and public support for concrete left-leaning policy positions belies a large disconnect between what passes for moderate policy positions among Congress and in the media on the one hand, and among the public on the other. This longstanding observation by scholars of public opinion (see Eismeier 1982 and Sanders 1988) still stands at odds with the median voter theorem, which would of course predict that politicians need to approximate the policy positions of the median voter in order to win the most votes. But it turns out that the median that candidates gravitate towards is quite distant from the median voter. Gilens and Page (2014) further cemented the reality of this disconnect by showing that the preferences of the public had no impact on policy when controlling for and comparing to the preferences of elites. It should be noted as well that MVT's conception of the median voter as unmoved does not allow for the possibility of voter learning, or correspondingly, "teaching" by political elites. Instead, the MVT is a rock around which the politician's ship must navigate, and this rock cannot be convinced to change its position by a rousing stump speech or an effective smear of the opponent.

The Puzzle

While the MVT has become a bone of contention rather than an article of faith in political science, despite all of its faults, the mythology of the median voter seems just as prominent as ever in the popular bloodstream of American politics. But why doesn't it work? After all, it is an intuitively appealing theory that works like a charm in the world of game theory and mathematical models. Downs (1957), drawing on Hotelling's (1929) work in economics, offered a classic explanation of American democracy on the basis of the assumptions of the median voter theorem, including rational office-seeking politicians, a rational voting public, and parties that are incentivized to come toward the center. Why exactly does such an intuitively appealing theory of democracy fail to correspond to reality? This is of course a major question in political science, and here I can only sketch the outlines of some of the more important answers given.

One major reason is that there are systematic distortions of the information that reaches voters about politics through a profit-driven media system owned by powerful elites (Bennett 1992, Ferguson 1995, Parenti 2011). Another is that people's psychological attachments to group identities (especially party identities) make it difficult for voters to spot the disconnect between their own preferences and the positions of politicians in the party they identify with (Tajfel 1981). The investigation of fandom in politics in Chapter One certainly bolsters this idea.

Though these considerations point to how this disconnect can go unnoticed by the public, they still do not explain why the disconnect occurs in the first place. While the MVT can't answer this question, different theories of electoral competition can. For instance, under the directional voting model proposed by Rabinowitz and Macdonald (1989), where voters exercise a less precise "push" in a leftward or rightward direction, rather than the "pull" they exert over policy under the MVT, this disconnect between median elites and median voters is theoretically consistent and quite plausible.

However, this theory still ignores key phenomena at the elite level. Ferguson's (1995) investment theory of party competition argues that the electorate only gets to weigh in after the class of large donors—what he calls the investor class—has already had its say. Others have called this the invisible primary, or money primary. Major campaign donors have a tremendous influence on which candidates are considered viable, and in the earliest phases of the campaign, media organizations commonly use money raised as a proxy for the viability of a given candidate. This, when combined with a meta-strategic focus on electability in November, only increases the long-term power of large, early donations.

So, if the MVT can't account for this most basic of observations about American politics—the power of big-money donors to influence candidate viability—why does it retain such popularity in political punditry?

The key answer, I believe, comes from a more anthropological and interpretive direction: the median voter creates meaning for Americans through its mythology. A myth in the proper sense is a story that situates our lives in a context of meaning. From an anthropological perspective, it doesn't matter if a myth is factually inaccurate or not—what matters is how well it serves this meaning-making function. When I refer to the *myth* of the median voter, it is not to make a claim about the empirical validity of the MVT, but to highlight the story it tells us about our politics. It tells a story about the ultimate sovereignty of the voter by situating the voter as the unmoved prime mover of politics to which elites and politicians are forced to respond. At the same time it ignores the powers of elites, such as the various ways they narrow down the field of candidates, influence politicians, shape the information presented in the media, and build loyalty to partisan political identities to keep voters in predictable and controllable patterns of behavior. The median voter theorem is just as important for what it ignores as for what it focuses on, and it systematically obscures these more undemocratic aspects of elections.

The Meta-Median Voter

It is important at this point to recall our earlier observation that even if the median voter theorem is not true, it still exerts a powerful effect on our politics *as a myth* merely if enough people—and especially if enough powerful people—*believe* it to be true. Since MVT is seen as common sense by so many pundits, more moderate candidates will be favored in most political analysis, giving them an advantage in terms of how they are treated by the media. So because enough powerful opinion-makers believe MVT to be true, it *becomes* true and its effects are observable, insofar as moderate candidates are systematically advantaged. When enough pundits, on the basis of the median voter theorem, declare Joe Biden to be the most electable candidate against Donald Trump, then he gets a boost from the media and thus *becomes* the most electable candidate in the primary as his name recognition and popularity climb. This happens not because MVT is accurate on its own terms, but because enough powerful people *believe* it to be. It is in this way that the median voter theorem functions as a self-fulfilling prophecy.

Whether Biden really was the most electable candidate is another question entirely, and one that is next to impossible to definitively answer, thanks to its counterfactual nature. In fact, electability itself may largely be a self-fulfilling prophecy, insofar as the public's impression of a candidate's electability depends on the media consensus about his or her electability. This is a large part of the problem with electability, which on its own is a reasonable expectation for a primary voter to have of a candidate.

Notice exactly how the meta-median voter operates to bring about the self-fulfilling prophecy of the MVT. Even if the median voter doesn't exist in any real sense, a meta-median voter—that is, primary voters who want to satisfy an imagined general-election median voter by selecting the most "electable" candidate as their party's nominee—can bring about the same results in primary elections. The myth of the general election median voter is enough to produce a primary meta-median-voter that can influence primary elections in a real way: whether MVT is true or not, the parties still pick candidates that converge toward the center.

It is also worth pointing out how this all functions to limit the scope of the politically feasible. The consistent effect of this is to pull candidates toward the center. Recall also how the gravitational center here is not the center of policy preferences among the public, as classical median voter theory would posit, but the center as defined by opinion-making elites in both parties, which, as discussed above, is consistently to the right of our best estimates of the median voter on most economic issues. Social and cultural issues are another matter, but it is easy to recognize that there are systematic differences between elite and popular opinion on these as well, arguably running in the opposite direction, although such issues don't as neatly map onto a left-right spectrum.

The Power of Myth

The median voter theorem must be characterized as a myth in the full sense of the word. To call the MVT a myth in this sense is not to criticize its empirical accuracy, although it is certainly subject to plenty of that sort of criticism, as we have seen. Rather, it is to recognize how the MVT tells us how to interpret our elections and imbue them with meaning.

The median voter theorem does this in several ways. First, it treats our elections as mathematical exercises, legitimating them with a veneer of science, calculation, and geometrical rigor. From an outsider's perspective, the whole of the political science literature on spatial voting and the median voter theorem can be seen as the technical working out of an electoral system that must clearly be judged better than any alternatives. If elections and voting are being studied so mathematically, so precisely, so empirically and so scientifically, then this gives the definite impression that any prior debates over how to set up an electoral system, or a political system more generally, have long been settled. The future of American politics is merely the honing and optimization of what we already know to be the best system. This is perhaps a more broad-ranging critique of mainstream political science in general, but it seems as incisive here as anywhere: the median voter theorem comes with a baked-in status quo bias. This also dovetails with an observation made in the previous chapter: strategic thinking typically limits our range of questions to those that assume we are playing the existing game and that that is not going to change. We thus avoid criticisms of the rules of the game, and instead seek to optimize performance and enforcement of the existing game and its rules.

Second, the median voter theorem treats the voter as the unmoved mover, the only true sovereign in our elections. The central dictum of the MVT is that parties must converge to compete for the median voter. It is clear who is calling the shots in this formulation. Political parties and political elites are merely adapting to the solidly set forth demands of the median voter, the prime mover. However, while the median voter is the anchor around which political elites compete in this theory, this voter is also inanimate and passive, and the object, not the subject, of strategy. The median voter's preferences are taken as a given, as a truly independent variable, and the origins and causes of these preferences are not interrogated. To be fair, the MVT is not completely incompatible with efforts to explain voters' preferences, but spatial theories of voting have long treated explanations for the voters' preferences as either *a priori* assumptions, or simply outside the scope of investigation. Seen from outside the discipline, this often appears as a tacit endorsement of the existing system as sufficiently democratic. If the voter is the ultimate authority to whom candidates, parties, and government must answer, and if the voter answers to no one else but her own preferences, this necessarily must be a democratic and just political system.

The outstanding irony here is that, if the imaginary general-election median voter is the prime mover, then the meta-median voter in a primary election is the one being manipulated, and that the outcome of strategic median-voter logic is not democratic but antidemocratic. Certainly there are many primary voters who, operating under the tyranny of strategy, vote in the primaries for their second, third or fourth choice, simply based on a belief that their own preferred candidate has a smaller chance of beating the other party's candidate. Such voters essentially run a simulation of the general election in their minds which tells them to override their own preference, even to falsify it, at the ballot box. This is a twisting of democracy. *The strategic logic of games here overrules the democratic logic of the polls.* Primary elections cease to be the reflection of the will of the people of the party, and instead become a reflection of the shared simulacrum of the outcome of an imagined November contest. The desires of the voter are overridden by the desires of *imagined others*. If the median voter theorem and its strategic use in primaries has wide purchase among the voting population, then this meta-strategic voting may explain in part why Americans so frequently feel that neither party represents them. Also, voters' expectations of candidates' electability are usually more malleable and manipulable by elites than are their more fundamental issue-based candidate preferences. This would suggest, ironically, that the more strategic the voter, the easier it is to "game" him. Indeed, one could argue that whenever a voter is led to vote against her own true preference, she has effectively been convinced to censor her own vote, to silence her own voice. In this case she does so merely for the sake of what she imagines *others'* preferences to be.

If such a voter is being gamed, then who is doing the gaming? Who convinces her to moderate her own vote to placate these imagined others? This is the third way that the MVT imbues elections with meaning: it crucially overlooks most of the undemocratic characteristics of our electoral system. Central to this is the recognition of the power of money in politics. The only real currency in MVT models is votes. Once money is brought into the equation, as in Ferguson's (1995) investment model, it has powerful effects that voters alone cannot muster: "only investors can compel... parties to take up an issue—because only investors can afford to pay the high 'replacement cost' of nonresponsive parties (candidates, etc.)" (p. 383). That is to say, only those with large sums of money readily available can afford to mount a real campaign challenge to an incumbent who is dissatisfactory to them. And since only parties and candidates who face a credible threat of challenge can be held accountable, then the investor class acts as a selectorate that decides which candidates can afford to run, and which candidates will get a strong challenger, before the voters decide on anything. This moneyed selectorate is able to effectively veto candidates before those candidates have the chance to make any appeal to the electorate: unless big money is funding your opponent, there is little credible threat of your being challenged and voted out.

On top of this, the information that voters receive through the investor-owned media is systematically filtered in particular ways that are anything but fair, complete, or accurate. Lastly, party loyalty and other powerful social identities structure voters' responses to the policy positions put forward by candidates. This is a strategy consciously used by parties and their flagship candidates to sway voters or keep them loyal, which diverts voters from policy concerns and instead toward concerns of electability and winning. In the central narrative of the median voter theorem, which tells us that voters are calling the shots to which political elites must respond, all of these powers of elites over voters go unmentioned.

Fourth, the MVT presents our elections as more or less fair contests between left and right. In assuming a public that is normally distributed along the left-right policy scale, it is presumed that one party will be converging on the center from the left, and the other doing the same from the right. But this overlooks a systematic bias to the right among political and economic elites in the arena of economic issues, which tends to push the bipartisan elite consensus to the right of the actual public preferences on economic policy. In terms of policy on social issues, there may be systematic elite biases as well, and generally to the left, particularly concerning immigration, gender politics, and other culture war issues.

Finally, the effects of the popularity of the MVT narrative can be real. As this chapter has argued, the median voter theorem can become a self-fulfilling prophecy. Through primary election concerns over electability, the MVT tends to produce the narrowed landscape of candidates that it predicts. It does this through the imaginary construct of the median voter, which need only exist in the minds of pundits and primary voters. Simply put, if primary voters merely believe that they need to satisfy the median voter in November for their party to win, that median voter has already become the sovereign, even if he is entirely imaginary.

It is here that we see the power of myths and narratives to shape concrete political outcomes. Regardless of the median voter theorem's normative and empirical failures as judged throughout the years by various scholars of politics, it retains its status as a structuring myth of politics in mainstream political discourse. Precisely because of this, it still exerts a powerful effect on the outcomes of elections. The logic of this self-fulfilling prophecy might best be captured in the immortal words of *Seinfeld*'s George Costanza: "It's not a lie... if you believe it."

Conclusion: The Median Voter and the Tyranny of Strategy

To return to the four main observations of the previous chapter, we can see how the median voter theorem analyzed here provides a case study of the pitfalls of an overly strategic approach to politics. First, we can see that the MVT tends to bring our analytical focus to elite competition for the median voter, in the meantime losing sight of more impactful questions of policy. For instance, when the MVT approach asks what policies candidates should advertise, this is treated merely as a strategic means to the end of getting elected, and not as a means to solve social problems or otherwise meet concrete social and political aims. Again, overly strategic approaches tend to lose sight of the value of the ends in favor of the means.

Second, we can also see how the MVT's narrow focus on how candidates can best compete in the existing electoral system serves to reify the established system. In this case it does this by assuming the voter to be the unmoved prime mover, the landscape around which parties and candidates must navigate. This paints an overly democratic picture of the political system, suggesting that there is no need to change the rules of the game.

Third, despite the centrality of the median voter, the MVT puts us in the shoes of the political elites who are competing, casting them as the heroes of the democratic drama, and engendering our empathy for their position. Meanwhile, social groups trying to achieve certain policies, or for that matter the voters themselves, are merely the stationary set pieces around which the candidates compete. Under MVT, strategizing is for the politicians, and thus our own strategic intrigue has us, the fans, putting ourselves in their shoes, perhaps even to the point of forgetting our own interests or that of the public at large.

Finally, and perhaps most clearly, the logic of the median voter theorem is readily wielded against candidates who put forward stronger proposals that would represent significant policy change, especially those that would threaten the investor class or well-established economic sectors. Senator Bernie Sanders' ambitious proposals in 2016 (most notably Medicare for All and a $15 minimum wage) were often called "pie in the sky" by critics, implying that these things were impossible, and that Sanders was being naïve and insufficiently strategic in how he approached these issues. In the same vein, arguments were frequently made that Sanders would be trounced by any Republican opponent because most Americans would see his proposals as too extreme. Similar arguments were made against

Donald Trump in running in the Republican primary in 2016. The undercurrent here is that if one has ambitious policy ideas, they should at least be disguised as more moderate, nuanced proposals, because the strategy of the political chessboard requires it. Under this reasoning, pushing straightforwardly for what you want, and trying to persuade the public that it will benefit them, is a simpleton's approach, like playing tic-tac-toe when your opponent is playing twelve-dimensional chess. In the end, the fact that Sanders was able to garner the support of significant numbers of voters who ended up voting for Trump in the 2016 general election certainly goes against the MVT's predictions, and even calls into question the overall utility of the left-right spectrum as a way to explain voter behavior.

The median voter theorem provides us with a kind of case study in how strategic approaches to politics can lead both analysts and voters astray, due in part to faulty assumptions, in part to a veneer of scientific and quantitative rigor, and—most interestingly—precisely because of expectations that imagined others in the future will think by the same logic.

Chapter Four

Resisting the Reign of Quantity

> *It would be nice if all of the data that sociologists require could be enumerated because then we could run them through IBM machines and draw charts as the economists do. However, not everything that can be counted counts, and not everything that counts can be counted.*
>
> —William Bruce Cameron

This book has made the case that there are good reasons for analysts not to conceptualize politics as a sport. The first overarching reason, discussed in Chapter One, is that many of the ills of modern politics stem from its fanification. Like rabid sports fans, the role of political partisans is to support their favorite band of elite players, even forgetting their own interests except insofar as they coincide with the team's interests. These political fans are emotionally attached to their political heroes to the extent that they not only identify with them but are alienated from those outside the fan club. All of this despite the fact that everyday people have much more in common materially with their presumed opponents down the street than they do with their elite heroes.

The second general reason, elaborated in Chapter Two, is that thinking of politics as a sport makes us prone to the tyranny of strategy. This can mean, for instance, an excessive focus on the strategic calculations involved in playing the game of politics, at the expense of an awareness of its unavoidable moral dimensions. A preoccupation with strategy can also keep analysts from critically interrogating the nature of the game itself, taking the rules for granted rather than questioning them.

Furthermore, the intricacies of political strategy are frequently cited by elites and political professionals in order to discredit and deflect straightforward pushes for popular policies. Elites frequently dissemble on the grounds of the arcane knowledge of strategy, dismissing popular opinion while saying to the public, "This isn't as simple as checkers; I'm playing a more advanced game of chess here." The third chapter showed how these things manifested in the 2016 Democratic presidential primary, around the concepts of strategic voting and the median voter.

This concluding chapter will draw out the broader implications of the overall critique of politics-as-sport, including social and political concerns about optimization, gamification, big data, and artificial intelligence. This chapter also connects the book's argument with thinkers such as Max Weber and René Guénon, in a critical analysis of what contemporary author Paul Kingsnorth calls "the Machine." We will see manifestations of these concepts in both sports and in politics. All of this adds up to a broader social trend that we might call quantified managerialism, and which represents a real threat to democratic institutions, customs, and habits of mind.

Quantification and Optimization: Algorithmic Management

In sports and gaming today, players and commentators often discuss performance using the language of optimization. You will frequently hear about "optimal" moves, and "correct" strategic decisions. The underlying assumption is that in any situation, there is one strategically best move, and any other move is calculably inferior.

Sports and games have not always been conceptualized in this way, but with the rise of computing power, it seems every game is now liable to be treated as an optimization problem, complete with calculus equations. In the second chapter, I discussed how this phenomenon manifested in baseball with the rise of sabermetrics: managers started to rely less on tradition, intuition, and their own experience, and instead relied on quantified metrics compiled into databases in order to determine the mathematically optimal strategic choice. This sea change has been highlighted in controversial instances of algorithmic management, such as Tampa Bay Rays' manager Kevin Cash's infamous decision to remove pitcher Blake Snell in the middle of a particularly strong performance in the World Series. But most of the time the datafication of baseball management has gone on unnoticed, largely since in most cases it does not controvert the established wisdom of management. But even in these cases, one consistent effect of quantified analytics is that it has transformed our view of games from an open field of creative possibilities into a narrowing search for the One Right Move.

In the chess world we have seen the same transformation. Moves in chess have always been described as "strong" and even "best" in many cases. But more recent (and more mathematized) terminology shows the furthering of this trend. Good moves are frequently called "optimal" or "correct," and slightly weaker moves will often be called "inaccurate" or "imprecise." It is not that such expressions were absent before the dawn of powerful chess computers—no, such language can be found in chess books from the pre-computer era—but such terminology is certainly more predominant now than in the past. These terms all imply the existence of One Right Move in any particular position, and that this move can be found if we just do the calculation. Such a way of thinking is certainly more common today, and became common as the strength of computer chess engines began to rival and surpass the strongest human players over two decades ago.

Now, the painstaking process of determining whether a move is strong or weak has been replaced by a quick click to turn on the ubiquitous chess engine. In the past, the two central components of thinking in chess—analysis of various lines of play, and the evaluation of resulting positions—had to be earned through the wits of the analyst himself. And they had to be put forward with some degree of confidence, as well as some degree of trepidation that others might uncover a mistake in the analysis. Or perhaps not a mistake, but an evaluative disagreement that could not be readily resolved by resorting to a computer output. As human products, these analyses were the result of hard work that built up one's own organic understanding of the game. They also naturally took into account human preferences for elegance, simplicity, practicality, clarity, teachability, drama, and beauty. Now, both analysis and evaluation have been largely outsourced to the black box of the chess engine, whose output is frequently taken as gospel.

Indeed, the engine is "correct" (by its own quantitative standard, at least) the overwhelming majority of the time, and can virtually always "see" farther than, and outplay, a human master. My point here is not that the chess engine is wrong, but that it has warped our view of the game as a human practice. Qualitative evaluations of positions have been collapsed into a plus or minus numerical score. Whereas a human might have said of a given position: "black is solid, but cramped, while white's space advantage and initiative give him most of the winning chances," today the computer, in a matter of seconds, spits out a "best" line of play and a number (say, +0.82) that can only be interpreted one-dimensionally as "white has a moderate advantage."

In 1951, notable chess writer I.A. Horowitz evaluated a particular position at the twenty-second move of a line in the Ruy Lopez opening:

> To all intents and appearance, white has the initiative. Black, however, is well poised for defense. With best play, a draw should result. A cardinal wit summed up

> the position succinctly with "Black will probably win. White's attacking chances will undoubtedly drive him into a rash action." (Horowitz 1980, p. 61)

When this same position is fed into Stockfish, the most popular chess engine, it says, tersely: +0.7. Certainly computer engine evaluation has been useful to the practice of chess. But it is an awfully thin evaluation which has nothing to say about what exactly is to be valued.

The same is now true for evaluations of players as well as positions. In the chess world, there have long been arguments and debates about just how strong the great players of the past were, compared to the top players of today. Perhaps because chess players are relatively uncomfortable with ambiguity and uncertainty, there are a variety of efforts to answer this question authoritatively through computer analysis. One common approach is to run all of the known games of an old master through a top chess engine, to see how the computer evaluates his moves relative to the moves it would make. This produces a statistic called "average centipawn loss," a simple negative number that shows the computer's evaluative difference between its move (presumed to be best) and the old master's move.[9] If the average loss is twenty centipawns, then each move by that player, on average, was 0.2 pawns "worse" than the computer's recommendation. What is interesting is that, by this measure, human players can by definition *never* come out ahead, since the "best" move is defined here *a priori* as the move the computer selects. This means that by this standard, the old masters could never—even once—have found a move that is better than the computer move. But this is of course ridiculous, as computers cannot even today play chess perfectly, which means that sometimes human players will find better moves than they, even if only by luck. Nonetheless, advocates of this method of comparison claim that it is objective (or at least much closer to objectivity), and thus superior to older methods, which typically compare players of different eras by how well they performed against their contemporaries. After all, such methods would get lost in the wilds of qualitative argumentation, lacking an authoritative number by which to settle the score.

By comparison with most games, chess is easy to quantify. This means it serves as a canary in the coal mine, so to speak. The transformation chess has undergone will continue to take place in other games and sports (like baseball), and in broader ways in society as well, as computers get more powerful and more versatile. We will be able to outsource more areas of life to algorithms, by letting the black box of the computer make difficult decisions for us, just as has been presaged on the chessboard.

Artificial Intelligence and Gamification

One example of this is a recent interview with Whitney Wolfe Herd, founder of the dating app Bumble. Herd eagerly anticipates a day when artificial intelligence can radically simplify the dating process: "There is a world where your dating concierge could go and date for you with other dating concierges… and then you don't have to talk to 600 people. It will then scan all of San Francisco for you and say, *These are the three people you really ought to meet*" (Harper 2024).

This is an extension of the logic of the chess computer: you don't have to do the hard work yourself; you need only set the computer to work and it will say, "these are the three top moves you really ought to consider." Given her enthusiasm for the project, one wonders why Herd stopped the winnowing at three people, rather than the One Right Person. If the quantitative wisdom of AI is better than one's own discernment, the logical endpoint, after all, is algorithmically arranged marriage. But taking the logic that far would upend the narrative of AI as an empowering force that frees us from drudgery. Algorithmically narrowing the field down to three *already* seems disturbing to most people, as it is clear that it removes drudgery only insofar as it removes human agency.

As the capabilities of computers grow, our own capacities, even those we've previously taken for granted as necessary for life, will atrophy. If data-driven AI can make all the major management decisions for a baseball team, what skills does a manager need? Sabermetrics obviates not only a manager's decision-making abilities, but also erodes his accountability. It's not only much easier to make a computer-recommended decision, but when things go wrong, the computer gives the manager a built-in excuse. The computer recommended the One Right Move, after all, and the manager can say he made it. Even if things didn't work out, he followed the best protocol: the One Right Move is always to listen to the computer.

Outsourcing decisions to machines alters the political landscape in these two ways. First, it depoliticizes and constrains a decision by quantifying it, such that there is a "correct" decision that must be made—all other options are, as gamers say, strictly worse, strategically speaking. The decision had to be made given the information at the time, and the optimal choice was made. The second consequence is that this removes accountability from the decision-maker, but only in one direction. When everyone defers in advance to the machine's judgment, a human authority figure can only be faulted for *disregarding* the computer's recommendation, not for following it.

There is a liberal proceduralist element here: the idea that institutions can be trusted as long as the process goes as planned. A criminal trial meets the standard of justice, and an election meets the standard of democracy, if and only if the prescribed procedures were followed properly. In the same way, as long as one follows the process of the statistically and strategically best computer-assisted decision-making, one can have done no wrong. In extreme cases, the computer simply says no, not allowing the human agent to make an alternate decision, and completely obviating accountability: "sorry, ma'am, the computer says I need a receipt to refund you for this item."[10]

We see here a new form of Frederick Winslow Taylor's scientific management. Taylorism was discussed in Chapter Three, but in the computer age its applicability and scalability are far greater than in the advent of the assembly line. Now, scientific management is ordained not just at the workplace, but also in games, and in every place in between.

The connection to games is often made explicit in the concept of gamification. More and more parts of everyday life are being gamified, which is to say that increasingly more things are being designed to induce a game-like state of mind, and game-like behaviors. Our lives are replete with examples, from the innocuous to the jarring, with many of them powered by the ubiquitous smartphone: language learning apps, meditation apps, dating apps, fitness apps, productivity apps, customer rewards apps, and a plethora of programs in all levels of education. Most notably, virtually all successful social media platforms now function essentially as games, which has led to the effective gamification of our social life writ large.[11]

There are obvious benefits to this trend, and gamification has enabled many to learn more and do more than they otherwise would be able. But we should not lose sight of the dangers. For one, it rests on the ongoing surveillance and quantification of all spheres of life, which accumulates large piles of data—often of a highly personal nature—over which large corporations have control. Another danger is that such games interact with us at least as much as we interact with them. In other words, the point of gamification, from a marketing perspective, is to make a product addictive, providing plenty of neurochemical hits to users in order to keep them coming back for more. While we play these games, we must realize that they are playing us. A third difficulty is the upscaling of competition that gamification often produces. This may seem innocuous enough in the context of language learning or fitness, but dating apps and social media have already radically transformed the social world along these lines.

The critique I want to make here is somewhat different than the above complaints, while also retaining parts of each. The idea of optimization inevitably creeps into gamification thanks to the necessary quantification of everything that is to be gamified. Once who you are can be summed up in a social media profile, or a dating app profile, it must be optimized for peak performance. Here we see a transformation not just of our behaviors but of our identities that we project out into the world. When we start thinking of our social life in these terms, we are no longer doing the optimizing but are ourselves being optimized. We are no longer instrumentalizing these online services, but are being instrumentalized by them, and we converge to a way of thinking about ourselves and about others that incorporates quantified metrics to a degree unprecedented in history. The impact of artificial intelligence on these trends has yet to be seen, but one sensible prediction—in keeping with the above example from the world of online dating—is that it will accelerate them.

But despite all the novel technology powering such social transformations, this is not all entirely new. Taylor's scientific management, after all, applied the ideal of the one most efficient technique (the One Right Move, in our terms) to the design of the factory floor in the late nineteenth century, and we can see a certain throughline running from this to our current era. The biggest figure on this throughline is Max Weber, a founding father of modern sociology.

Weber on Rationalization

Writing in the early twentieth century, Weber identified an ongoing process that he called rationalization. As George Ritzer summarizes: "According to Weber, formal rationality means that the search by people for the optimum means to a given end is shaped by rules, regulations, and large social structures. Individuals are not left to their own devices.... In a formally rational system, virtually everyone can (or must) make the same, optimal choice" (Ritzer 2013, p. 30). Weber saw the rise of bureaucratic rationalization under capitalism as a creeping force that threatened human freedom, a concern that is best expressed by his metaphor of the "iron cage" of rationalization:

> When asceticism was transferred from the monastic cell to the life of the calling and moral concern with this world began to predominate, this helped to create that powerful modern economic world, bound to the technical and economic conditions of mechanical production, which today shapes the way of life of all who are born into it...with overwhelming pressure... In Baxter's view, concern for external goods should lie on the shoulders of the Saints only like 'a light cloak, which can be thrown aside at any moment'. But fate has allowed that cloak to become a casing as hard as steel [alternate translation: *an iron cage*].... The external goods of this world have acquired an increasing and ultimately inescapable power over men.
>
> (Weber 1905, quoted in Runciman 1978, p. 170)

For Weber, human life was being gradually restrained by the iron logic of efficiency and optimization. He looked on the development of Taylorism and scientific management as a harbinger of a totalizing logic that would not liberate us but shackle us to the one right way of doing something. He saw in the logic of Taylorism something inherent to capitalism, and something that would break free from the merely economic sphere and reorient our lives toward the true north of optimization.

Interestingly for our purposes here, Weber critiques rationalization by evoking a connection to sports explicitly in the very same paragraph: "In the United States, where [the fulfillment of one's calling] has been given most freedom, acquisitiveness, stripped of its religious and ethical meaning, tends today to be associated with purely competitive passions, which often give it the character of a sporting contest" (Weber, p. 171). Here Weber points out rationality's lack of real human depth by noting its resemblance to a sports mentality, where the unquestioned aim is to win, and the only question is how best to ensure that one does.

Rationalization essentially gamifies one's approach to life, and Weber sees this as an impoverishment of life itself, which is of course much more than a game. More than this, rationalization confines us within a framework of living that is spiritually bankrupt: "it might indeed become true to say of the 'last men' of this cultural development: 'specialists without soul, hedonists without heart: this cipher flatters itself that it has reached a stage of humanity never before attained'" (p. 171). As one who hesitated to "enter the domain of value-judgments," these are strikingly condemnatory words from Weber.

The Reign of Quantity and the Machine

More recently, writer Paul Kingsnorth has sounded a similar alarm. Kingsnorth calls upon twentieth-century philosopher René Guénon's idea of the "reign of quantity," the idea that modernity is pushing humanity toward a quantitative, mechanistic, and materialistic understanding of the world. As Kingsnorth interprets Guénon:

> Nothing that could not be measured would now be accepted as real. This had led inevitably to the reign of 'profane science', 'mechanism leading to materialism' and an 'inversion of correspondences' in which all traditional values, rooted in spiritual unity, were turned upside down. The profane was worshipped, and the holy was profaned.
>
> (Kingsnorth 2022)

For Guénon, quantity is the opposite of unity, meaning, and spirit, and thus the reign of quantity is a dissolution of all of these.

The reign of quantity and the death of the spirit, as ethereal as it sounds, is concretely manifest in the world of sports. Recall how the data-based decision-making of sabermetrics has seemed to most baseball fans to violate the spirit of the game. This was made especially vivid in the decision to replace the pitcher Blake Snell in the World Series. The essence of football seems to be violated by a head coach in the last moments of a game deciding, based on mathematical probabilities, to go for an immediate win-or-lose 2-point conversion rather than sending the game to overtime by kicking an extra point. A deep and beautiful winning idea being executed on the chessboard by a master—it goes against the spirit of chess for a lesser player to call such a move "suboptimal" only because his computer found another move it prefers. If Guénon is concerned in the abstract with quantification hollowing out the spiritual life, then these are clear examples of quantification hollowing out the spirit of sports. The world of sports provides a clear window into the "profane science" of quantity which so concerned Guénon.

How does this translate into politics? Is there a spirit of politics that is hollowed out by quantity in the same fashion? Certainly the proper spirit of politics, if one can speak of such a thing, is more ambiguous and contested than the spirit of sports. But the ideal of democracy represents a reasonable modern consensus for how politics ought to work. Here we can point back to examples from earlier chapters to illustrate how treating politics as a sport hollows out the cherished ideal of democracy.

As discussed in Chapter One, treating politics as a spectator sport empties democracy of its meaning, as does the fanification of politics that results from this. When citizens are assumed to be passive spectators in a contest between two predetermined teams, democracy is thinned out. When they loyally root for their team to the extent that they are impervious to reasonable counterarguments, and when they lose the ability to discuss politics outside of their fan group, democracy is impoverished.

Similarly, the tyranny of strategy leaves democracy as a shell of its former self, as argued in Chapter Two and Chapter Three. When the emphasis on strategy precludes ethical discussions and deeper questions about the rules of the game, when it makes people care more for the competing political elites than for everyday people like themselves, it diminishes democratic capacity. And when the strategic complexity of the game of politics is cited as a reason to dismiss popular policies on the grounds that politics is too nuanced for the unwashed masses, the democratic principle is certainly diluted.

In sum, fanification and the tyranny of strategy both, in various ways, twist the essence of democracy into something much less. These can all be seen as examples of the hollowing out of the spirit of democracy. Guénon's concept of the "great parody" in which the institutions that claim to preserve valuable traditions (such as democracy) are merely dead shells of the real thing, also rings all too true in our current political moment. We do not need to offer an elaborate discussion of what democracy is in order to point out that these ways of thinking move us away from the ideal. The spirit of democracy, like the spirit of sports, is worth preserving, but the forces of erosion—corruption, institutional rot, and the ideological winds of fanification and strategic quantification discussed in this book—are strong and unrelenting.

Kingsnorth, writing in our current moment, has a more evocative term for Guénon's reign of quantity: The Machine. According to Kingsnorth, "we have not junked a sacred order for a profane one. We have instead enthroned a new god, and disguised its worship as the disenchanted pursuit of purely material gain. We have dressed up as a mere 'economy' our new idol and sovereign: the Machine" (Kingsnorth 2021). Drawing on Lewis Mumford, Kingnorth says that the Machine is not merely the accumulation of its literal machine parts—factories, cars, the internet, and all manner of technology—but instead is "a tendency within us, made concrete by power and circumstance, which coalesces in a huge agglomeration of power, control, and ambition" (2021).

The Machine is a system that organizes both social relations and how we think about them. Its characteristics include: centralization, bureaucracy, a sense of inevitability, and a permanent imperative to expand, even to globalize and universalize itself. Some of its central driving values are efficiency, individualism, liberation from limits and from the past, commercialism, naturalistic materialism, and a scientism which claims to be able to scientifically determine what we ought to value. Progress is its central myth: the future will necessarily be an improvement on the past.

The Machine can be thought of in Weberian terms as rationalization's latest expansion, with efficiency and control becoming the organizing principles of not just work, but politics, social life, and recreational life as well, and all on a global scale. According to the Machine, with efficiency and control comes progress, and all of these are quantifiable and visible in the data.

Both fanification and the tyranny of strategy, as applied both to sports and to politics, exhibit characteristics of the Machine. In the case of fanification, we can see how turning people into loyal spectators with a distaste for discussing politics with fans of the other team has made politics more quantifiable, more efficient, and more controllable from the perspectives of the elite teams and their owners. The same goes for the tyranny of strategy, which makes both political elites and everyday citizens think about politics as a machine would, thinking about how to optimize political strategy to achieve given ends, rather than thinking whether those ends ought to be given in the first place. And both these trends push everyday people to question their own capabilities and to instead defer to putative experts, even mechanical ones.

The contention of this book is that we should be wary of any understanding of politics that has us thinking like fans, or like machines. The politics of democracy calls for the cultivation of human virtues: engagement with both allies and adversaries, tolerance for ambiguity, and an ethic of critical citizenship. It is not a spectator sport to be managed by powerful institutions, and it is not an engineering problem to be solved by computerized optimization. It is qualitatively different—and much richer—than either of these.

Endnotes

1. https://www.ncaa.org/about/resources/research/estimated-probability-competing-college-athletics
2. https://www.hsph.harvard.edu/news/press-releases/poll-many-adults-played-sports-when-young-but-few-still-play/
3. e.g., https://www.nationalreview.com/2020/12/the-case-against-2000-dollar-relief-checks/
4. I have elaborated on this particular argument in Darr, Ben, "The Power to Say No: How Voter Shaming Inverts Democracy," *Midwestern Marx*, January 22, 2021.
5. Orfalea, Matt. "Kamala's KHive trolls boosted by bots while media defends harassment campaigns." *The Grayzone*. April 16, 2021. Available at: https://thegrayzone.com/2021/04/16/kamalas-khive-trolls-harassment/
6. The aphorism was later widely used, especially by Green Bay football coach Vince Lombardi, to whom the origin is often misattributed.
7. No more than three of the FEC's six commissioners can be from the same political party. Interestingly, in recent years, due to resignations of commissioners the FEC has had difficulty meeting its quorum of four.
8. Alexandria Ocasio-Cortez, Pramila Jayapal, Ilhan Omar, Ayanna Pressley, and Rashida Tlaib at this time were typically seen as the most progressive members of Congress, and thus the main members of "the squad."
9. Chess engines evaluate positions by estimating which side is "up" by how much. For most engines, the unit for how much is the pawn, the chess piece of the smallest worth. The computer is not simply counting who has more pawns in a crude material sense but is treating "pawns" as a unit of advantage. If the evaluation is greater than +1.0 (or less than -1.0 for an advantage to black) then white has an advantage

that can probably be converted to a win with best play by both sides.

10. Credit is due here to David Walliams, who made famous the catchphrase "computer says no" on the UK television series *Little Britain*.
11. For a list of notable examples of gamification, see https://xperiencify.com/gamification-examples/.

References

Abercrombie, N. and Longhurst, B.J., 1998. *Audiences: A sociological theory of performance and imagination*. Sage.

Aden, Roger C. 2007. *Huskerville: A Story of Nebraska Football, Fans, and the Power of Place.* Jefferson, NC: McFarland.

Barrett, Grant. 2006. "Fan Service." *The Official Dictionary of Unofficial English.* New York: McGraw-Hill.

Baym, Nancy. 2000. *Tune In, Log On: Soaps, Fandom, and Online Community.* Thousand Oaks, CA: Sage.

Bennett, Lance. 1992. *The Governing Crisis: Media, Money, and Marketing in American Elections.* New York: St. Martin's.

Bishop, Bill. 2009. *The Big Sort: Why the Clustering of Like-Minded America Is Tearing Us Apart.* Mariner Books.

Brady, David W., Hahrie Han, and Jeremy C. Pope. 2011. "Primary Elections and Candidate Ideology: Out of Step with the Primary Electorate?" *Legislative Studies Quarterly* 32(1): 79–105.

Broh, C. Anthony. 1980. Horse-race journalism: Reporting the polls in the 1976 presidential election. *Public Opinion Quarterly*, 44(4), 514–529.

Busse, Kristina, and Jonathan Gray. 2011. Fan cultures and fan communities. *The handbook of media audiences*, pp.425–443.

Cameron, William Bruce. 1963. *Informal Sociology: A casual introduction to sociological thinking.* New York: Random House.

Click, Melissa. ed., 2019. *Anti-fandom: Dislike and hate in the digital age*. NYU Press.

Converse, Philip. 1964. "The Nature of Belief Systems in Mass Publics." *Critical Review* 18.

Darr, Ben. "The Power to Say No: How Voter Shaming Inverts Democracy." *Midwestern Marx*, January 22, 2021. Online at https://www.midwesternmarx.com/articles/the-power-to-say-no-how-voter-shaming-inverts-democracy-by-ben-darr.

Debord, Guy. 1967. *The Society of the Spectacle.* Translation by Fredy Perlman and Jon Supak (Black & Red, 1970; rev. ed. 1977). Online at Library.nothingness.org.

Downs, Anthony. 1957. *An Economic Theory of Democracy.* Harper and Brothers.

Drier, Peter. "Most Americans are liberal, even if they don't know it." *The American Prospect,* Nov. 10, 2017.

Edelman, Murray. 1989. *Constructing the Political Spectacle.* University of Chicago Press.

Eismeier, Theodore J. 1982. "Public Preferences about Government Spending: Partisan, Social, and Attitudinal Sources of Policy Differences." *Political Behavior* 4: 133–45.

Ferguson, Thomas. 1995. *Golden Rule.* University of Chicago Press.

Fiorina, Morris. 1999. "Whatever Happened to the Median Voter?" Paper prepared for the MIT Conference on Parties and Congress, October 2, 1999.

Gilens, Martin, and Benjamin I. Page. 2014. "Testing Theories of American Politics: Elites, Interest Groups, and Average Citizens." *Perspectives on Politics* 12(3).

Gray, Jonathan. (2003). New audiences, new textualities: Anti-fans and non-fans. *International journal of cultural studies, 6*(1), 64–81.

Gray, Jonathan, Cornell Sandvoss, and C. Lee Harrington, eds. 2007. *Fandom: Identities and communities in a mediated world.* NYU Press.

Gwinner, Kevin and Scott R. Swanson. 2003. A model of fan identification: Antecedents and sponsorship outcomes. *Journal of Services Marketing.*

Harper, Tyler Austin. 2024. "The Big AI Risk Not Enough People Are Seeing." *The Atlantic,* May 21, 2024. Online at: https://

www.theatlantic.com/ideas/archive/2024/05/ai-dating-algorithms-relationships/678422

Hassell, Hans J.G. 2018. "Principled Moderation: Understanding Parties' Support of Moderate Candidates." Legislative Studies Quarterly 43(2).

Hedges, Chris. 2009. *Empire of Illusion.* Nation Books. Online at: https://theanarchistlibrary.org/library/chris-hedges-empire-of-illusion

Herman, Edward. S., & Noam Chomsky. 1988. *Manufacturing consent: The political economy of the mass media.* Random House.

Hersh, Eitan. 2017. Political Hobbyism: A Theory of Mass Behavior. Online at: http://www.eitanhersh.com/uploads/7/9/7/5/7975685/hersh_theory_of_hobbyism_v2.0.pdf

Hill, Seth J. and Chris Tausanovitch. 2015. "A disconnect in representation? Comparison of trends in Congressional and public polarization." *Journal of Politics* 77(4).

Hinck, Ashley. 2019. *Politics for the love of fandom: Fan-based citizenship in a digital world.* LSU Press.

Horowitz, I.A. 1980. *How to Win in the Chess Openings.* New York: Cornerstone Library.

Hotelling, Harold. 1929. "Stability in competition." *Economic Journal 39.*

Iyengar, Shanto, Helmut Norpoth, & Kyu S. Hahn. 2004. Consumer demand for election news: The horserace sells. *The Journal of Politics, 66*(1), 157–175.

Jenkins, Henry. 1992. *Textual Poachers: Television Fans and Participatory Culture.* New York: Routledge.

Jenkins, Henry. 2006. *Convergence Culture: Where Old and New Media Collide.* New York: NYU Press.

Kingsnorth, Paul. 2021. "Blanched Sun, Blinded Man." Online at: https://paulkingsnorth.substack.com/p/blanched-sun-blinded-man.

Kingsnorth, Paul. 2022. "In the Desert of the Real: After the Western Deviation." Online at: https://paulkingsnorth.substack.com/p/in-the-desert-of-the-real?s=w.

Kunda, Ziva. 1987. Motivated inference: Self-serving generation and evaluation of causal theories. *Journal of personality and social psychology*, *53*(4), 636.

Lewis, Michael. 2004. *Moneyball: The art of winning an unfair game*. WW Norton & Company.

Mason, Liliana. 2018. *Uncivil Agreement: How politics became our identity*. Chicago: University of Chicago Press.

Mayhew, David R. 2004. *Congress: The electoral connection*. Yale University Press. First published 1974.

McCulloch, Richard. 2019. "A Game of Moans: Fantipathy and Criticism in Football Fandom." In Melissa Click, ed., *Anti-Fandom: Dislike and Hate in the Digital Age*. NYU Press.

Montagnes, Brendan Pablo and Jon C. Rogowski. 2015. "Testing Core Predictions of Spatial Models: Platform Moderation and Challenger Success." *Political Science Research and Methods* 3(3).

Olsen, Henry. "Trump's greatest threat has arrived." *Washington Post*, April 25, 2019.

Parenti, Michael. 1986. *Inventing reality: The politics of the mass media*. St. Martin's Press.

Parenti, Michael. 2011. *Democracy for the Few, 9th Edition*. Wadsworth.

Patterson, Thomas E. 2016. News coverage of the 2016 presidential primaries: Horse race reporting has consequences.

Postman, Neil. 1985. *Amusing Ourselves to Death: Public Discourse in the Age of Show Business*. Viking Press.

Putnam, Robert D. 1988. Diplomacy and domestic politics: the logic of two-level games. *International Organization*, 42(3), 427–460.

Rabinowitz George, and Stuart Elaine Macdonald. 1989. "A directional theory of issue voting." *American Political Science Review* 83(1).

Redlawsk, David. 2002. Hot Cognition or Cool Consideration? Testing the Effects of Motivated Reasoning on Political Decisionmaking. *The Journal of Politics* 64(4): 1021–1044.

Ritzer, George. 2013. *The McDonaldization of Society. 20th Anniversary Edition*. Sage.

Romer, Thomas, and Howard Rosenthal. 1979. "The Elusive Median Voter." *Journal of Public Economics* 12(2): 143–170.

Runciman, W.G., ed. 1978. *Weber: Selections in Translation*. Trans: Eric Matthews.

Saad, Lydia. 2017. "US Conservatives Outnumber Liberals by Narrowing Margin." Gallup. Online at: https://news.gallup.com/poll/201152/conservative-liberal-gap-continues-narrow-tuesday.aspx

Sanders, Arthur. 1988. "Rationality, Self-interest, and Public Attitudes on Public Spending." *Social Science Quarterly* 69: 311–34.

Sandvoss, Cornell. 2003. *A Game of Two Halves: Football, Television, and Globalization*. London: Routledge.

Sandvoss, Cornell. 2005. *Fans: The Mirror of Consumption*. Cambridge: Polity Press.

Sandvoss, Cornell. 2013. "Toward an understanding of political enthusiasm as media fandom: Blogging, fan productivity and affect in American politics." *Journal of Audience and Reception Studies* 10(1): 252–96.

Solomon, Norman. 2007. The military-industrial-media complex. *Democratic Communiqué, 21*(1), 60–71.

Stokes, Donald E. 1963. "Spatial Models of Party Competition." *American Political Science Review* 57(2).

"Strategy on GOP 2016ers." Attachment to an email from the Podesta emails. *Wikileaks*, 2016. Online at: https://wikileaks.org/podesta-emails/emailid/1120

Suskind, Ron. 2004. "Faith, Certainty, and the Presidency of George W. Bush." *The New York Times Magazine*. Online at: https://www.nytimes.com/2004/10/17/magazine/faith-certainty-and-the-presidency-of-george-w-bush.html

Taibbi, Matt. 2021. *Hate, Inc. Why today's media makes us despise one another.* OR Books.

Tajfel, Henri. 1981. *Human Groups and Social Categories.* New York: Cambridge University Press.

Theodoropoulou, Vivi., 2007. The anti-fan within the fan: Awe and envy in sport fandom. *Fandom: Identities and communities in a mediated world,* pp. 316–27.

Tufekci, Zeynep. 2018. "How social media took us from Tahrir Square to Donald Trump." *Technology Review.* Online at: https://www.technologyreview.com/2018/08/14/240325/how-social-media-took-us-from-tahrir-square-to-donald-trump/

Wann, Daniel, and Nyla P. Branscombe. 1990. Die-Hard and Fair-Weather Fans: Effects of Identification on BIRGing and CORFing tendencies. *Journal of Sport and Social Issues* 14(2): 103–117.

ACADEMIC AND SPECIALIST

Iff Books publishes non-fiction. It aims to work with authors and titles that augment our understanding of the human condition, society and civilisation, and the world or universe in which we live. If you have enjoyed this book, why not tell other readers by posting a review on your preferred book site.

Recent bestsellers from Iff Books are:

Why Materialism Is Baloney

How true skeptics know there is no death and fathom answers to life, the universe, and everything

Bernardo Kastrup

A hard-nosed, logical, and skeptic non-materialist metaphysics, according to which the body is in mind, not mind in the body.

Paperback: 978-1-78279-362-5 ebook: 978-1-78279-361-8

The Fall

Steve Taylor

The Fall discusses human achievement versus the issues of war, patriarchy and social inequality.

Paperback: 978-1-78535-804-3 ebook: 978-1-78535-805-0

Brief Peeks Beyond

Critical essays on metaphysics, neuroscience, free will, skepticism and culture

Bernardo Kastrup

An incisive, original, compelling alternative to current mainstream cultural views and assumptions.

Paperback: 978-1-78535-018-4 ebook: 978-1-78535-019-1

Framespotting

Changing how you look at things changes how you see them

Laurence & Alison Matthews

A punchy, upbeat guide to framespotting. Spot deceptions and hidden assumptions; swap growth for growing up. See and be free.

Paperback: 978-1-78279-689-3 ebook: 978-1-78279-822-4

Is There an Afterlife?

David Fontana

Is there an Afterlife? If so what is it like? How do Western ideas of the afterlife compare with Eastern? David Fontana presents the historical and contemporary evidence for survival of physical death.

Paperback: 978-1-90381-690-5

Nothing Matters

a book about nothing

Ronald Green

Thinking about Nothing opens the world to everything by illuminating new angles to old problems and stimulating new ways of thinking.

Paperback: 978-1-84694-707-0 ebook: 978-1-78099-016-3

Panpsychism

The Philosophy of the Sensuous Cosmos

Peter Ells

Are free will and mind chimeras? This book, anti-materialistic but respecting science, answers: No! Mind is foundational to all existence.

Paperback: 978-1-84694-505-2 ebook: 978-1-78099-018-7

Punk Science

Inside the Mind of God

Manjir Samanta-Laughton

Many have experienced unexplainable phenomena; God, psychic abilities, extraordinary healing and angelic encounters. Can cutting-edge science actually explain phenomena previously thought of as 'paranormal'?

Paperback: 978-1-90504-793-2

The Vagabond Spirit of Poetry

Edward Clarke

Spend time with the wisest poets of the modern age and of the past, and let Edward Clarke remind you of the importance of poetry in our industrialized world.

Paperback: 978-1-78279-370-0 ebook: 978-1-78279-369-4

Readers of ebooks can buy or view any of these bestsellers by clicking on the live link in the title. Most titles are published in paperback and as an ebook. Paperbacks are available in traditional bookshops. Both print and ebook formats are available online.

Find more titles and sign up to our readers' newsletter at www.collectiveinkbooks.com/non-fiction

Follow us on Facebook at www.facebook.com/CINonFiction